Carp are Jerks

Mark Usyk

Copyright 2019 Mark J Usyk

All Rights Reserved

This book or any portion thereof may not be reproduced or used in any manner whatsoever without the express written permission of the publisher except in book reviews.

Cover art by Sean Usyk

Edited by Get It Write Editing and Self-Publishing

First printing 2019

Acknowledgments

Writing a book is a personal endeavor, but it's rarely done without the help of others, either directly or indirectly. Without a Grandfather who took an impatient 5 year old to an old friend's pond to drown worms, there may have never been the passion that led to writing fishing stories. Without *friends*, both new and old, many of these stories would've never taken place just the same as the fish wouldn't have been caught. So to everyone I fished with during the time frame it took to finish my second book, whether you find yourself in a story or not, thank you.

To everyone who offers words of encouragement, this book is for you. Let's face it. As much as I claim to write for myself, I honestly write equally just as much because you ask for more and I'm happy to have supporters at my side. Thank you also.

And finally, the fish. If it were not for you hiding under logs and behind boulders in rivers, I might never venture out into the wilderness and experience the wonderful things I have in the places you live. Perhaps the greatest thank you should go to you, the very reason behind my storytelling. May your waters be full of oxygen and bugs, and may you sip at the surface long after man has faded from existence.

Fishing is much more than fish. It is the great occasion when we may return to the fine simplicity of our forefathers.

-Herbert Hoover

Contents

Forward

Introduction

1 Home Waters	12
2 Patience	17
3 Mohawk War Paint	21
4 Carp	25
5 Moments of Balance	37
6 Fly Rods Are Not Found In The Lawn Care Dept. Take 2	40
7 Wet Elk	43
8 Hail Mary Casts	47
9 Steelhead	50
10 Brook Trout	69
11 No Hope	84
12 Dry Flies	98
13 Green Lake	101
14 Haircuts	114
15 You Can't Catch Fish with Lawn Mowers	119
16 All Things Fly Fishing	123
17 Black Flies and Lost Boys	130
18 Western NY Speculations	135
19 Guiding	144
20 Bass	167
21 Head Waters	181
22 Matters of Importance	198
Epilogue	203

Foreword

Mark recently asked me to write the "foreword" to his latest book. It is an honor and a privilege to do so....

In doing so I have to tell you a bit about Mark, as he's truly my best friend. I know this because I've never gotten mad at him. I've never fought with him. I haven't even gotten frustrated with him, even when he catches dozens and dozens of fish in front of me. Because of this, I guess Mark is the best-ist friend. Mark will drop everything on the spot if I need help. Although he doesn't act like it, he's wise. He also knows he's wise, because he's a writer and story teller. He is humble wise.

This is similar to how the best comedians are extremely intelligent. You have to be in order to be quick and witty. You have to be wise in order to write a good story and relish in the memory and also use great prose to make something as boring as walking down a trail or picking up trash at your favorite fishing hole interesting. Mark does this very well. I often wonder what's going through Marks head when he's experiencing something. Is he writing it in his head or just observing? I can tell you that Mark takes his writing seriously, because I've been in the car with him while he's taking notes... or we'll see a car in front of us with a funny bumper sticker and he'll quickly grab his little flip notebook and jot something down, only to be brought up later in some creative context.

So Mark asked me to write a "foreword" but it really is a "backward". (Mark will love this....) It's a "backward" because this book is number two of many I hope Mark writes, and this book is a good reflection back to a part in his life that has defined him. At least the *him* he is today. He was the metal former, blacksmith, cell tower climber, factory worker guy... and now he's not just a fisherman; he is a *storytelling fly fisherman*.

What you'll find in this book is a transformation of a man who has gone thru change from what some would call tragedy. Look, it's out there... Mark went thru a divorce and he made it clear that he did because Mark doesn't hide much. Because that's what Mark does, he says it like it is. Mark isn't the guy who makes up stories to hide the truth. Mark is an author who explains the truth in a way that makes life seem more interesting. Life *is interesting*, and Mark's reflections back on some times he went fishing and what they meant to him isn't only interesting, it's insightful.

In this book CARP ARE JERKS, the title tells it all the way it is. Typical Mark Usyk Style. Not Sugar coated... perhaps embellished a little. He writes his stories how he would like to see them played on the big screen. And if you know Mark and the type of movies he loves, he would also make a great director.

I have been extremely fortunate to be Marks sidekick in life and in many of his stories. I'll admit, I get really excited when he writes a book or a story, because I often skim it right away looking for two letters; JP. He tends to put me in a nice light in his stories as the guy that goes fishing with him. I now know what it's like to be Chewbacca, and it's awesome. I get to play a part in Marks life and therefore I always make it to the screenplay in his stories. Han Solo and Chewy... Peas and Carrots... That's pretty awesome.

So please enjoy CARP ARE JERKS. Because 1.) They *are* jerks... and 2.) This book goes well beyond just fishing stories... they're life stories of a guy that holds a fly rod a lot. Read this book like you're watching a great movie. Read it once for the story and read it twice, three times or more and pause once in a while to really observe and notice little things that the director intended you to see. You did a great job on this one Mark. And thank you for letting me be your sidekick, hand photographer and friend.

Jordan P. Ross

JP Ross Fly Rods

Introduction

When I was in the hot rod and custom car scene, there was something I used to say about the owners of the cars on a regular basis. "No one will ever like your car as much as you do." The meaning is better understood with some context to put it in.

Car people tend to go on and on about how much work they put into their rides. About how much horsepower they make, how fast they are, how much money they spent, how much time is in them. They'll go on and on about every detail for as long as you'll let them. I'm not saying I couldn't have talked about my '55 Chevy for hours...I did. What I mean is, no matter how much someone loved their car, whoever they were trying to impress was never going to love it nearly as much. To the owner, it was something very personal. To the listener, it was just another nice car.

Fishing can be a lot the same. If you catch a great fish, you want to tell everyone about it. But no matter how big it was, the person you're trying to express the excitement and importance it had on your life to just *isn't* going to feel the same thing inside. To you, that fish was personal. To them, it's just another fish story. Most anglers love fish stories, but that's all they are when they aren't your own...just another story.

Writing about something may be the only way to make something that's personal to *you* become just as personal to someone else. Allow me to explain.

I stood in the river, the current passing around my knees and continuing downstream as if I didn't even matter to it. It may have been named a river, but here it couldn't have been more than twenty feet wide at the most, and over along the far cutout bank draped in exposed tree roots it couldn't have been much deeper than four feet or so.

I thought to myself how it was more of a creek or even a big stream than a river. I made my cast above a submerged tree trunk upstream. As the streamer sunk and drifted past, I gave the rod tip a little wiggle and added some life to the feathers and rabbit fur tied to the size twelve hook, in hopes that I'd fool a fish in the shadows and slack water under the trunk. In my mind's eye I saw my streamer looking like a struggling and weak bait fish, half swimming and half drifting in distress. An easy target. A free meal.

It passed unmolested. It made its way past the waterlogged dead fall that I was so sure held an ambush of bronze scales and continued on downstream, finally swinging across the current and coming tight at the end of my line. I stripped it back to me, my eyes scanning the water. Up and down stream I picked apart the currents and eddies, the cover, the pockets, looking for another spot in which I'd feel sure there'd be a smallmouth lying in wait.

Two hours later as I broke down my fly rod at the Jeep, I considered the day. It was still a fine day spent immersed in nature. And even in failure there were still lessons to be learned.

To me, writing those four paragraphs was personal. Because I lived them. But because I chose to write them, they became personal to the reader as well. Every reader saw something different in their mind. What *they* wanted to see. This is why, as good as the movie might be, the book is always better.

Every reader stood in a different creek. The creek they wanted to stand in. Every reader cast a different streamer. The streamer they wanted to cast. Every reader saw a different sunken tree. The tree they wanted to see. Every reader saw the creek bottom, the water, the surroundings, all of it in their minds, and not one looked the same as anyone else's. If I did what I do right, every reader was there, but not in my creek, not in my waders. They were there in *their own*. The telling of the story through writing made it personal for both the writer and the reader.

It wouldn't have had quite the same power if it had been *spoken* as opposed to written. For one thing, I don't know anyone who would tell a story verbally exactly the same way they would describe it when written. No one gets descriptive enough to do the same when they're talking, and if they do, they're thought of as long-winded, and probably a little over dramatic.

If you'd been there as I walked back to the Jeep and witnessed me falling over backwards while trying to pull my waders off, you might've asked me how the fishing was. Those same four paragraphs I wrote would've come out of my mouth a lot simpler... *"I got skunked, but it was a good day to be out."*

And this is why I write, and why I write about fly fishing.

1

Home Waters

It's a section of water less than a mile long, the tail end of a thirty-something mile creek that runs south to north smack in the middle of New York State. One I claim as my home water. Most people have some kind of home water, whether it be a creek or river or even just a small pond. And for those who don't and never have, I feel truly sorry. It's the type of thing that shapes a childhood, has the ability to direct a life, or in the least gives one fond memories to cling to in the hard days of growing up and becoming *responsible.*

With a home water at least in your past, there's always *the old days* and how good they used to be. On my home water, I caught crayfish in the fourth grade by the dull light of my grandfather's flashlight, fished unsuccessfully for trout as a teenager, and made my first jump from a bridge guardrail into questionable depths to impress a girl, among other too numerous to count random misadventures.

Which is why - when I agreed to move my family from the small old house across the road from the dairy farm out into the country years ago to this little slice of what I fondly refer to as suburbia hell - that I ever agreed to live with neighbors to my right and left at all in the first place. Looking out the kitchen window was my home water. Ironically, it was the farthest downstream point I'd ever fished on it. Moving into this house was almost like an excuse to pick up where I'd left off years ago. The very spot on the blue line on the map, to be exact.

The first time I explored this new stretch of the creek, as downstream as it gets before it gently mixes with the Mohawk River at a good bend of its own, I think I was something of a spectacle walking through town. It's nothing to see kids down at the bridge in the middle of town with spinning rods and worm buckets trying their luck in the *town pool* as I like to call it. Or to see them in pairs riding down the sidewalk, fishing rods held across handlebars and a look of concern on their faces as they pass fences and trees, the bikes bouncing and jerking to the left or right on upheaved concrete squares, hoping to avoid catching the rod tips in chain links or worse, seeing someone walking in their path. But I became very aware that a guy in waders with a nine-foot fly rod was something of a spectacle.

That first spring day, and into the first months, dogs in picture windows alerted their owners to a stranger passing, sideways glances were fixed in my direction from the seats of riding lawn mowers, and smokers standing outside our town's only bar would question how the fishing was while giving me a look like someone who'd unknowingly stumbled onto a nude beach full of senior citizens. They didn't really care how the fishing was, but it seemed that they had to say *something*.

It's funny how things change. Years later kids stop on the bridge and watch me cast deer hair poppers to the shaded far bank for bass and ask me what they're hitting on. The guy on the mower nods and raises a hand in a neighborly wave and after I published my first book, we held a book signing at the town bar. People actually showed up, and they *really did* want to know how the fishing was.

But the creek. The fishing. The first time I explored this last leg, I couldn't believe it was the same creek. Where over most of its distance the creek is known as our areas best trout stream, down here in the last of its currents the creek snakes back and forth between two corn fields, cutting through sandy earth known as *The Flats*. Here, the bottom is gravel and sand. Gravel out in the open where the current washes it clean, and sand in the deep pools and in the pockets behind the downed willow trees and the old tractor tires here and there. Tires washed downstream from farmers' junk piles of the past to form artificial current breaks and they act like boulders and pocket water, much in the way naval ships are sunken to form artificial reefs in the ocean. It isn't pretty, it isn't natural; but when you find them in the water, you use them the same as you would a boulder or tree trunk. You cast to it.

Here, I found ten-foot-tall walls of sand and roots, flanking the water on both sides in some places; no way in the water or out except to wade from up or downstream. And in these places, where the light brown sandy walls met the creek's current, just below the surface, there seemed to be a constant ledge where the water could no longer carry away the earth grain by grain quite so easily. And along that ledge is where I'd find the pot of gold, or more accurately, *bronze*.

On some days that first year, it seemed like there was a smallmouth anywhere from the size of my hand to sometimes longer than my forearm at the end of just about every cast. And when the smallmouth didn't fall for my game, a fall fish was there to take its place.

The fall fish is nothing but a big minnow, but I've argued that they fight every bit as hard as the smallmouth. I don't know that they do it naturally or if it's something brought on by man, honestly. They're the red-headed stepchild of our streams, and I have a suspicion that they fight so hard out of anger; not from being hooked, but from being regarded as a *trash fish* - or worse yet, always being confused with creek chubs and suckers. They may just be trying to prove a point. I get it. And I'm happy to have them put a bend in my fly rod all the same.

That first year, I also came the closest that I ever have *so far* to hooking myself. I was casting a small streamer, really getting in a rhythm, and I suppose getting a little cocky now that I'm looking back. I'd make the short cast upstream and across, work the streamer along the ledge, half-dead drifting it and half jerking it ever so slightly, doing my best to imitate a dying bait fish; when it reached the bottom of the short run, I'd lift it out of the water and slingshot it back up to the top in one fluid motion. Now that I replay it in my head, yeah, I was getting cocky.

On about my fifth or sixth cast, the streamer grabbed my hat, took it right off my head, and deposited it into the water at my feet. I stared down at the ball cap as it sank in a foot of water, the streamer hooked in the dirty white netting of the back of the hat. I raised my right hand to feel my head. I didn't feel any *pain*, but I've got a lot of scars from stupid stuff, and most of those scars started out with an open wound and no pain. But at least there wasn't any blood on my hand.

I picked up the hat, ripped at the fabric as the barbed hook came free, shook the water off and placed my soaked hat back on my head. A new scar for my hat, none on my scalp. My casting slowed down, my cockiness subdued by how close I'd come to catching myself, and then I heard my uncle's voice in my head.

My uncle was never a fisherman that I remember, but he *was* a biker when I was young. And when his son and I had bought our first motorcycles, he'd passed on some wisdom hoping it would slow us down a bit and keep our heads on a swivel. "Boys, you've either *been* down or you're *going* down." I quit riding before I ever went down, but his words suddenly became relevant again that day while fishing. I figured it's the same with hooking yourself.

It has been too long playing with fish hooks; I'm forty-three now, so we'll say thirty-something years. So, I'm beginning to pinch down the barbs on every hook regardless of what I'm casting to. *Momma didn't raise no fool*. Of course, that depends on who you ask. Don't ask my ex-wife, or the fish for that matter. And there are a couple of old employers, some old coworkers, and a couple deer in the woods I'd ask you not to consult, either. I guess now that I think about it, there's a possibility momma *did* raise a fool, but it's not her fault. Some of us, no matter our upbringings, are our own worst enemies.

Forty-three years? I guess I'm about due. I've been told that's how insurance companies work. "Oh, you haven't had an accident in thirty years? Well then, you're high risk. You're about due." But I guess if I'm due, my home water is as good a place as any for it to happen. Not that it's going to hurt any less.

2

Patience

When things finally come together, they feel like a fish pulling against you at the end of your line...

Patience. By definition, it's the capacity to accept or tolerate delay without getting angry or upset. My grandmother used to tell me it was a virtue. As a high school kid in ripped jeans and a leather jacket, it was the only hit song off the Guns N' Roses *"Lies"* album. And today, twenty-some-odd years later, patience is something I seem to be in short supply of. Whatever it is I want done, I don't want to screw around, I just want it done now. It *needs* to happen now, so that I can move on to more important things. Like *fishing*.

The only place I could find my last remaining bit of patience anymore was on the water with a fly rod. And, more often than not, I was finding it harder and harder to get there. Where everything else seemed to wear my patience thin - errands to run after work, getting the boys to baseball practices on time, loading and unloading the dishwasher when I just wanted to get to writing, or flies that need to be tied - there was always something else to do.

The rattling exhaust under the Jeep in the morning and the rushed and frantic tightening of the clamp holding it in place to silence it was another perfect example of something that would send my blood pressure boiling so easily. The only place left where I could find my patience was at the end of a looping fly line.

So, the irony? Well, that was when I could *finally* get through all the crap that life can throw at you as a parent, as an adult with a job and responsibilities, as an assistant Little League coach at the beginning of the season, and as the owner of a seventeen-year-old vehicle that could sometimes have its little *hiccups*. Once I got past all that and found an hour to string up a rod and walk out back to the creek, I'd find the creek blown out; still up from all the spring run-off. It seemed like it would never come down, never clear up. Chocolate milk forever.

And then one night, just as the last hues of reds and purples were filtering through the trees hiding the horizon, and just as the full moon was illuminating everything in a pale blue, I saw the fish. I happened to be idling the Jeep across the bridge over the creek in town on just *one more errand*. Normally, if there's no one else on the road, I'll almost always slow down, if not completely *stop* just to take a look. In the day time you might catch the dark shape of a decent carp on the sand flat of the inside bend, or the splash of a smallmouth as it chases a meal. But so far that spring, the water had been high and brown.

I couldn't see the color of the water in the moonlight, but I knew from only an hour earlier that it was still brown; so my idling across the bridge wasn't so much me looking for signs of life as it was me pleading with the creek in my own head to just *hurry and clean up already.*

I guess that's why it shocked me when I saw the fish jump. It was a bass. I know this because the silhouette was perfect; the fish had no detail except the crisp and exact silhouette of a smallmouth against the moonlight's reflection on the water.

The Jeep was barely moving across the bridge, so it didn't take much more than me hastily tapping the brake pedal to bring it to a sudden stop. If it wasn't for the seatbelt, I'd have probably bounced my head off the windshield. I took it as a sign. Clear water or not, the fish had to eat - and they were ready.

The next day after work, I found myself leaning against the chain link fence of the baseball field watching the boys warming up in two lines facing each other, just playing catch. The sun was finally warm on my face, bugs actually hovered above the grass, and mosquitos bit at my calves. *Finally*.

While the boys warmed up, I was thinking about that fish the night before, and at some point it became apparent to me that the sound of baseballs slapping leather gloves sounded an awful lot like bluegills smacking bugs off the bottoms of lily pads. I swatted another mosquito and came to the realization that there'd be no time to fish for a few days still. That bass at the bridge knew it. That's why he jumped. Smallmouths are trouble makers. They love to egg you on.

On Easter morning, my wife, Holly, was lecturing me in the kitchen about my lack of patience. This time because of the strict diet I'd been put on only days earlier by a doctor who'd informed me that I had an inflamed esophagus, ulcers, and a hiatal hernia. Apparently, when a doctor tells you that you need to take care of yourself, they *actually mean to take care of yourself*. It's not like when you see someone out somewhere and they say 'take care of yourself' as a way to end the conversation politely. Who knew?

The doctor who told me to avoid dairy for ten days (a test for lactose intolerance) and anything spicy for the rest of my problems; anything with sauce, anything citrus or carbonated; coffee and *even beer* among other stuff for who-knows-how-long. I was griping that morning about having to drink *not-milk-milk* with my Cap'n Crunch and having to avoid anything with flavor all together, and she was giving me the old "I know you don't have any patience, but you need to have patience while your insides heal up" speech. Then she asked me if I was going fishing.

I sat patiently and read some of John Gierach's new book while Holly went for a run. Now that I think about it, reading about fishing is probably about the only thing outside of fly fishing itself - or tying flies, or writing about fishing and tying flies - that can slow my mind down and settle my impatience.

When Holly got back, my impatience returned and I was struggling into my waders, getting mad about the time it was taking to rig up my rod; just generally continuing to act impatient. If there's one thing I'm good at, it's looking on the dark side of everything. If there's another, it's having no patience.

Everything I was doing was taking *too long*. I had Holly drive me over to the bridge up the creek a little ways because I didn't want to waste any more time walking. As she pulled away, I hopped the guardrail and hurried down the embankment and tripped through a patch of saplings. Then I stumbled across the rocks at the water's edge, crossed the mouth of a tiny feeder creek, and cursed at the mud trying to suck the boots off my feet, slowing me down. I finally found myself standing on the bank of a slow run just below some good riffles. It felt like it took forever to get there.

The water wasn't perfectly clear, but it was *beginning* to clear up. *Finally*. I could make out about two feet of visibility, and I figured that was about as good as I was going to get. I didn't have time to wait for it to get better. My patience waiting for the water to clean up was gone.

I made two false casts because three would have taken just too damn long, and I let the black cone-headed Woolly Bugger sink and drift downstream out of sight in the deep run. I wiggled the end of the fly rod, watching the energy transfer down the line, as much to give the bugger some life because my impatience told me I had to do *something*. The line paused and I lifted the rod tip. The rod bent and did a little dance, and a fish fought at the other end. I forgot about nothing going my way and about everything taking too long. Time stood still.

3

Mohawk War Paint

An edited version of this story originally appeared in the spring 2017 issue of *The Drake magazine*.

I had planned on driving up north to fish for brookies in the Adirondacks, but the week had been pretty hot, and the water levels were all low. I figured I better leave them alone and chase something a little tougher, a little less temperamental. I end up doing that a lot during the summer.

In the summer, the smallmouths are always ready to brawl, just waiting for someone to look at them cross-eyed, to say something about their mother, and I'm always willing to hurl an insult at them if that's what it takes. So after almost not getting up at the sound of my alarm because I thought it was getting me up for work, and after getting a weird look from a kid with a neck tattoo and stretched-out ear lobes behind the counter at the gas station (just because I bought a donut while wearing my waders), I was paddling down the Barge Canal in my canoe.

Just about anything that swims in New York State can be caught in the canal, save for the brookies I'd wanted to chase. I imagine any trout that end up in it do so by mistake, and don't last long. The high predator count and low oxygen levels aren't exactly conducive to trout. Even though there are so many different fish to be had, it's my least favorite water to fish. It's straight. Forever straight. Boring. It reminds me of the time I drove across Texas. You can see something on the horizon, but you never actually get to it.

Flanked on both sides by a wall of green, a shallow fog rolled and lifted in wisps off the surface and below the fog on the water laid a blanket of seeds and pollen from the Poplar trees. It looked as though a crop duster had dropped a load of sock lint. The sooner I got off the canal, the better.

I was in my Radison canoe, a light-weight job with oar locks so that you can row it like a john boat (which is pretty handy for trolling), if you're into that kind of thing. I like it because it's a ten-foot canoe that only weighs twenty-nine pounds, which makes it easy enough to carry from the Jeep to the canal about a hundred yards from the parking lot; but it's still nothing I'd ever consider hiking into off the beaten path ponds with.

On a side note, I met one of the owners of the Adirondack Canoe Company once when I was doing a guest speaker thing at an event down in the Catskills. He was showing me one of his composite canoes - a gorgeous thing - and he said it only weighed something like seventeen pounds. I asked him what the farthest portage was that he'd ever done with one of his boats and he told me five miles. But then he told me what I had suspected on my own, without needing anyone to tell me; no matter how light it is, after five miles, seventeen pounds may as well be seventy. I chuckled in agreement. Five miles with a pack on and a canoe over your head...think about *that*.

On the canal, the fog was rolling only inches off the water, and there was a splash on my right, about where the oar pushed water. By the time I spotted it, the huge snapping turtle was in the swirl left by the oar behind me, staring at me through the fog as if deep in thought. Then it ducked its head back under the water, and its massive shell followed. I had to wonder if it had tried to grab the oar - maybe thinking it was a duck or something - or if by chance, I'd almost swatted it as I passed by. I wondered what it would have done if it had actually gotten a hold of the oar. Its head was about the size of a softball.

I bumped the nose of the boat against concrete, the top of the dam on the side of the canal where the Mohawk River left the canal, and once again became its own current flow, meandering across the flats at its own pace.

I carried the canoe down the gradual slope of the dam face, almost losing my footing twice. I imagined myself sliding down, tearing the ass out of my Simms. In my mind, I could see the aluminum boat barrel rolling, ejecting paddles, fly boxes and Gatorades like a rally car shedding its parts and pieces in a spectacular wreck. But with a couple of four-letter words, and wedding party dance moves, I saved it. I pushed off at the bottom, fly rod at the ready. It didn't take long; three casts and I was into a fish.

The first fish came hard from a dark hole next to an eddy and fought the fight that all smallmouths fight; hard, full of fury and to the very end. It was wearing its war paint, slashes of brown against a backdrop of bronze. And through the next few bends in the river, they kept coming just that easy. Every three or four casts, there was an underwater melee just above the darkness.

The streamer would slap down and start to sink; maybe I'd get the chance to twitch it, strip it once or twice, or maybe they didn't have the patience to wait for evidence of life. But two or three smallmouths would launch at it, jockeying to get there first. Sometimes I'd skip the slab of feathers underneath overhanging brush, taunting the branches to try and grab it before the fish, and there again a ruckus would break out. It seemed too easy, like skipping all-beef patties to farm-raised sharks.

And then it just stopped. It could have been the two ducks that I pushed up river. Every time I'd come around another bend, there they'd be and there they'd go; flapping and thrashing to take off, wings beating water for thirty or forty feet, disappearing around the next bend only to repeat it all over again.

Inconsiderate bastards. But they were only ducks, so I couldn't hold it against them. Maybe the bass sent a warning down river ahead of me.

An educated angler could've perhaps made some type of notable observations on temperature changes, the angle of the sun, the phase of the moon…who knows. Well, not me, that's for sure. It's just one of those things that happens when you're fishing. It's the whole reason behind those bumper stickers about bad days of fishing being better than good days at work.

It had been two weeks since I'd been fishing before this morning. All because of that very thing. *Work*. Sitting on the portage yoke, drifting along on the current, my 7wt at my side like a revolver on the hip of an outlaw at high noon, I began to contemplate calling in sick the next day. Forever.

4

Carp

Some things are worth doing because they're easy. Like paying someone to change your oil, for example. Now I understand that any self-respecting man changes his own oil, I do. But it's entirely possible that I'm just not a very self-respecting guy these days.

Proof? Besides paying someone to change the oil in the Jeep? I let my own health go downhill for so long that I finally told myself I *had to see a doctor.* I couldn't eat or drink anything without getting almost immediate heartburn, and to get it to calm down enough to even think about going to sleep I had to eat a handful of antacids. Then I'd end up waking up a couple hours later going for another handful so I could get back to sleep. Anyone with respect for themselves and their body would've seen a doctor a lot sooner.

The final straw was realizing that I couldn't even finish a single beer before it felt like I was dying from being exposed to some type of chemical warfare agent. And I can't stand to waste a good dark beer. So, believe me when I tell you the night I couldn't finish that porter, I knew I was in trouble.

The next morning, I was waiting in the Jeep with the engine off while a kid in the pit below drained the oil. They tried to talk me into an air filter and radiator flush, and at that point I realized I was somewhere in the lower bowls of self-respect. I texted Holly that we should probably make me a doctor appointment.

Somethings are worth doing because they're easy - like paying someone to change your oil - while other things are worth doing because they might allow you to live a little longer. And living a little longer means you get to fish a little longer.

As far as the oil changes go, I changed my own oil for years. But what I found is that paying someone else to do it saves me time, the hassle of getting rid of the old oil, and I ruin less of my favorite t-shirts. It's also one less thing to take time away from fishing. Hell, I can get it changed in fifteen minutes *on the way* to the lake.

As for the whole doctor thing, they stuck a camera down my throat and told me I had a severely inflamed esophagus, ulcers, and a hiatal hernia. I figured it could be worse because somewhere at that moment, someone was being told they had cancer. But then they gave me a new diet and I figured maybe it really *couldn't* get much worse. Basically, if it had any flavor, it was off limits. You don't realize how much you like food until you're not allowed to eat it. But they said with time, meds, and the new diet, that I'd heal, so I guess sometimes late *is* better than never.

But if there are some things that are worth doing because they're easy, and some that are worth doing because you just can't live like that anymore, then you have to recognize that there are also some things worth doing *because they aren't easy*...which makes them all the more rewarding - like fly fishing for carp.

I don't care what you think about how challenging trout can be, because they're nothing compared to carp. When you're talking about the challenges of carp, those challenges are usually surrounded in frustrations and four-letter words...at least in the beginning.

For the most part, when it comes to trout - if you're talking about dry fly fishing a river - you spot the rises, you choose the right color and size of fly, you drift it over the fish, and you hope it falls for it. And it's no surprise when it does, it's no surprise when it doesn't; but even when it doesn't, you might at least get that last second refusal. You at least moved the fish...maybe. And you try again. Maybe a different pattern, but you know if the fish is going to eat or not, maybe after a couple casts. Carp? Carp will make your brain itch.

I never really dedicated myself to chasing carp, but I did try a couple times here and there. I even hooked into one once that towed me down river in my canoe before tangling me in a submerged tree. I had no other choice other than to just break it off at that point, a feeling of sadness I've never quite been able to completely shake.

You think you want to catch one when you see how big the things are as they cruise by, or as their tails break the surface while they're rooting around for something on the bottom. But if you thought you wanted to catch one just because you saw them, then there's no doubt in your mind that you absolutely *need* to catch one after it has peeled line and taken you and your fifteen-foot Coleman canoe fifty yards down river as if it was a Rottweiler chasing a cat while dragging an old lady down the street still holding tight to the leash. And you're praying the cat either climbs a tree or has a heart attack and dies, because she knows there's no other way that dog is stopping.

Shortly after I got the word from the doctor that I couldn't eat anything that was worth eating, the spring thaws had finally ended, and the waters began to clear up to decent and fishable. I had managed a few browns in a spot upstream from the house on the Oriskany Creek a week earlier - first on a black bugger and then on a little size eighteen brown dry fly - and once you catch the first fish of the new season, you just feel like it should keep rolling on.

It was great to be out and finally catching fish, especially after a long winter and a thaw that didn't let the waters come down for a good month. If a watched pot never boils and a watched clock never changes, then let me tell you, a blown-out creek that you watch daily from your kitchen window takes *absolutely forever* to clean up.

I was torn on how I should feel about the trout, though. They were from a little run that I hadn't caught anything on in the past two years, so there was that. But I was ninety-nine percent sure they were stockers because their scales were beat up pretty good, like they'd been crowded in concrete raceways, and all of them seemed to be almost the exact same size - about twelve inches.

I figured I hadn't caught anything there in a couple years because people always fished it hard from opening day on, and stringers of fish were always leaving from the spot. As a matter of fact, I normally avoided the place until summer when all the yahoos that left beer cans and empty snelled bait hook packets lying on the banks had moved on to the lakes and ponds to do their damage elsewhere.

So, it only reasoned that I'd caught fish there this year because the water had been junk - high and brown for the past month - and it looked like I was the first one to fish it so far. There was no trash and no boot prints. In other words, I beat the stocking truck chasers because they just hadn't bothered yet.

The problem with spring isn't just waiting on creeks to settle down, it's Little League. Right about the time that you can start to see the rocks a couple feet down in fading brown creek water, is about when Little League season kicks off. With a seven-year-old in minors and a twelve-year-old in his last year of majors - and you being the assistant coach - baseball is about to rule your life until the end of June.

Fishing becomes that thing you wish you had time for and when you do get to do it, it's for short periods of time when the conditions aren't so great because they were bad enough to cancel a practice or a game. You stand in a river casting with the rain falling in buckets telling yourself it doesn't affect anything because the fish are already wet.

Making matters worse would be the fact that the creek runs right by the ball field - only about twenty feet off the back corner of left field to be exact. You're right there and you can't do anything about it except try to explain to another six-year-old that if he doesn't get his glove up in front of his face to catch that ball, he's going to lose his teeth. This has nothing to do with fly fishing which only makes it much worse than it needs to be.

You can only have so many practices right there next to the creek before you finally decide to take control of your life, if only for a couple hours on a Saturday morning, and drag yourself out of bed when the sun is coming up. Of course, you have to watch your time, because walking out of the trees in shorts and old sneakers with a fly rod in your hand, to find out you're late for a game (and this in front of all the other parents sitting on the bleachers) is somewhat of a reputation builder. Of course, there are worse things you can be in life other than undependable.

I approach carp the way I approach just about any other fish I might catch or attempt to catch; that is, I go out to fish, tie something on that might get the attention of the types of fish that I know live there, and then hope for the best. If I catch what it is I'm hoping for, cool. Great. If I don't, oh well…chances are I caught something else, or in the least, spent time on the water enjoying the day and not mowing the lawn or some other waste of usable daylight.

When I decided to try and catch a carp on the fly, I really didn't have much more of a plan than when I tried to catch anything else. I tied on a rabbit zonker of one color or another and hoped that I could imitate a leach, figure out how they wanted it presented to them, and with any luck, firmly plant the hook in their mouth. How hard could it be? After all, I could catch trout, couldn't I?

Eight out of ten times, a trout will *at least* look at your fly, even if it doesn't eat it. It might do *more* than just look at it, even if it doesn't eat it. You might get the satisfaction of moving that fish, which might also be followed by the unsatisfactory last second refusal...the one where the fish makes a splash and you lift your rod tip thinking you're about to set the hook, only to realize the trout actually rolled and slapped the fly with its fin, the way a coach slaps his players butt on the way into the dugout after striking out early in the first inning. He didn't fall for it, but you can say to it in your best Pee-wee Herman voice *"Made you look!"*

Carp, while they may eat many of the same things a trout would eat, *do not* act like trout. Carp have got to be the spookiest fresh-water fish going, and they're not dumb, either. In fact, they're so smart they love to snub you out of what I believe is principle alone. If a trout is supposed to be some type of a sophisticated game fish, well then...*carps are jerks*.

When fly fishing for carp, more times than not it is over before the first cast even happens, if you're not mentally prepared. What I mean is, if you're not trying to sneak to the water's edge, or better yet trying to cast from behind a tree or hidden in the weeds, they'll probably see you and it's *game over*. It can be frustrating to see them only after they've seen you and they're on their way out of town.

The next place things can go wrong in a hurry is the cast. There's not much to say here that's never been said before. They're there, you make a cast, and they're gone. I've made plenty - thousands of bad casts to trout. Fishermen tend to exaggerate, yes, but that's probably pretty accurate. But even after spooking a trout because of a bad cast, you can many times give that fish a few minutes and try again and have a shot at it if the second cast is on the money. Carp? My experience is you only get one shot to make a perfect cast. The line slaps down, they're gone. The line shoots over their head, they're gone. And he's not coming back. *And,* he's probably going to tell his friends.

If you're good enough to get within casting distance, and you're good enough to make a gentle cast, then the third place it can all go wrong is with the fly. Or more honestly it's all in the carps head, the way I see it. I've had anglers tell me they use this fly or that fly religiously for carp. And the same ones have told me exactly what I've experienced countless times thinking I just sucked. It's not always the fly, sometimes that carp is just going to turn its nose away from anything you throw. Remember, they're jerks. And other times they'll surprise the hell out of you and take the last thing you thought would ever attract a carp's attention.

I'll never forget the first one that really blew my mind. It was out back on the creek in about thigh-deep water. It was raining, and I was fishing for smallmouth bass...*not carp*. But isn't that when the most spectacular things normally occur on the water?

I'd been doing well the last couple of days with the bass, using a simple black bunny leach pattern tied on a short shanked 1/0 hook. I'd wrap the shank with some flashy olive dubbing, then send a couple green strands of flash off the back end, and finally tie on two lengths of black rabbit strip opposite of each other - one on top, the other on the bottom - with a small black hackle wrapped behind the hook eye.

"Just some crap glued to a hook" is what I'd always tell people when they asked what I was fishing with. Sometimes I got the feeling they thought I was trying to keep secrets about what patterns I used, but the few guys who really know me knew I pretty much meant it literally when I said it. None of this is very serious to me, which is kind of the *whole point*. The only thing I take very seriously at all with fly fishing is *not taking it seriously*.

That pattern had been working well on the smallmouths, enough so that I had actually tied four of the same in one sitting which is, most of the time, pretty unusual for me. My short attention span and lack of seriousness usually has me tying one or two of some random patterns I typically pull out of my ass before I decide I want to try something different. And a lot of times I tie flies the same way I write. I don't have any real direction when I start, and I never know when I'm done until it just seems that there's nowhere else to go with it.

I was out on the creek that day after work, and after the baseball season had come to an end, with that exact rabbit strip streamer. It had been raining most of the day and I'd been looking out windows throughout the work day wondering if it had been raining hard enough or long enough yet to muck up the water.

So when I drove home, I made a pass over the bridge before my street and was pleasantly surprised to see that while the water was higher by a few inches, it was still clear. I made a U-turn on the other side of the bridge like I was in some high-speed car chase in a movie and hauled ass up the street to my house where I ran through my front door and came running back out my garage door with my 6wt in hand and my ball cap full of streamers on my head. It was carried out at about the same speed as Superman changing in a phone booth. So if the neighbors were watching, they were either impressed or thought I really had to go to the bathroom and my toilet must have been out of commission as fast as I was in and out and disappearing into the tree line behind the house.

While the water wasn't coloring up yet like chocolate milk, it was raising and noticeably cooler than the day before. I figured if the water coming up didn't affect the fishing, then the dropping water temperature most likely would; but I was making as many casts as I could get in, anyhow. You can't catch a fish if your line isn't in the water.

I was standing in the middle of the creek in waist-deep water and casting upstream and to the left bank, working a spot that was covered with overhanging trees. About my forth cast, I let that rabbit strip leach pattern sink to the bottom, then picked up the pace from the last three strips and gave it some *quick* strips. When it reached the edge of what I considered my target area, I picked the line up off the water to go straight into my back cast, and suddenly out from that spot I'd pummeled with casts comes a carp who was pouring on the speed like a dog running to the edge of its yards as if to chase off a kid on a bike. *I figured I'd spooked it* and it was taking off.

As the streamer left the water and sailed over my right shoulder, that fish turned from facing me head-on to cruising about fifteen feet in front of me down stream, and I saw that it was about as long as my leg. I may not be a tall guy - I might get the brunt of the short jokes now and then - but that's still a big fish. For whatever reason, since the streamer was already in the air anyway, I changed its direction as the line straightened out over the water behind me and sent it downstream ahead of the fish. I knew it wasn't going to make a difference; that carp was just going to keep cruising on out of sight. But I had to know in my mind that I at least did *something*. And then *it* did *something*.

The streamer plopped down about thirty feet down-stream and I just let it sink. As it was on its way down, that carp made a hard-left turn in its direction and poured on the gas. About the time I lost it under the reflection on the surface, I was thinking to myself that it must've been right about where the streamer was touching down on the bottom. Then the line went tight, the rod bent and tried to wrench itself from my hands, and I managed to get out "*Oh my G…*" as the leader passed its maximum weight capacity and my strip of rabbit fur and 1/0 Gamakatsu hook were gone forever.

I wasn't making quiet and gentle casts. I wasn't slowly dragging a crayfish or leach pattern across the bottom, and I was fairly close, standing right in the middle of the creek crunching on rocks and gravel. I was doing everything wrong, and then that carp did that. *Carp are jerks.*

If you stand on the bridge over the creek, you look down on a slow and deep gradual bend, and on the inside of that bend is a large muck flat were all the silt from upstream gets deposited. The bridge is the perfect spot to observe and think that you can figure these lumbering scaled monsters out.

The muck is a mostly colorless texture; there's not many other ways to accurately describe it, really. It's not brown, but not quite gray, either. Crayola would have to add a new crayon color called *"muck"* to match it correctly; they just don't have anything exactly right for the job. It's bare, except for all the pock marks from the carp nosing around searching for food. It's pock marked as far and deep as you can see it, and on a good day if you stand very still on the bridge for a while, you'll get to see them from a birds-eye view. I've counted as high as thirteen scattered across the flat during one spying session.

It's really something to watch a large carp feed from above. You're looking down on a teardrop shape of scales and a huge tail that makes you think of mermaids as it waves in the current the way a thin silk bed sheet waves in the wind. They concentrate inch by inch. It's not like they're just cruising around trying here, and then trying there, to root up something tasty. They're working like an archeologist works in a four-foot square and works over every inch of it with a fine-tooth comb before moving on.

When they really get to rooting around the way a wild pig does in a field, they tip up...their tail breaches like some delicate underwater plant, and the rest of their body disappears in a billowing cloud of silt.

Watching this really made me confident that if I could put something on that flat in front of them, I could get them to eat it. I could catch one on the fly. So, I began a campaign of carp angling and nothing else that lasted four consecutive days, and I learned some more. Mostly I learned that no matter how smart you think you are, *carp are jerks*.

I don't know how many times I placed some buggy-looking thing in a manner that I thought was just right, only to get the cold shoulder. I even found the proof - in my mind, anyway - that I was fishing the right pattern, *matching the hatch,* so to speak.

Every time I sat on my porch and pulled off my water shoes and then my neoprene socks, after wading across that muck, I'd find a small black leach about an inch long on my ankle. I knew where I was picking them up because I'd never had a leach issue on the creek until I started sinking in that muck up to my knees trying to leave the creek.

It was obvious to me that those leaches were one of the things the carp were eating, so I tied some inch-long black leaches and started fishing them, thinking I was really brilliant. I don't know too many people that have ever thought they were brilliant because they were constantly pulling leaches off themselves, but I'm here to tell you that in at least one circumstance, it can make you feel smarter. Until you cast them trying to catch a carp on a fly rod. Then you feel stupid again, because the damn fish are so smart.

If I landed them where I wanted to, and if the line landed gently on the water, and if my patience was in good shape to let it lie there on the bottom until a fish was close enough to spot it - but not so close to immediately spook it - a fish just might end up staring it down - moving in closer for a better look before it turned and continued looking around for something else.

I swear they'd look at it just to make me feel like a fool, knowing the entire time that they were never going to eat it. They were just screwing with me from the get-go. Or maybe they'd even bump it but not actually pick it up. But most of the time they never went that far. They'd pass it by like someone in a crowd walking past someone they knew and not giving them the time of day, pretending they never saw them. All the while watching them out of the corner of their eye as they passed. *Carp are jerks.*

5

Moments of Balance

Every now and then, I run across a fisherman who's all about how many fish they caught on a given day. Or catching only big fish. Or only trout. Or only bass. Something specific that when not achieved, sours their attitude on the water. It makes them gripe and complain...or even worse yet, turns them into cocky, arrogant, and egotistical blowhards. They could be the best angler I've met in a long time - possibly ever - but as soon as they start making excuses for why they're not catching the biggest fish, or why they aren't catching enough of them, or complaining about the creek chubs and pan fish that keep taking their flies, all their knowledge loses most of its merit in my head.

Likewise, when they start bragging and belittling other anglers because they don't catch as many, don't fish for the right fish, or the right way; you know, when they must tell everyone they meet how *great* they are, then all the knowledge they might actually have is - in my mind - lost. Meaningless. It means little to nothing simply because they've missed the most important part of it all. And that part has nothing to do with the size of a fish or the number, with perfect casts and the ideal fish.

Once, at an old job, another coworker spotted the stickers on the back window of my truck and the rod vault on the roof and he hunted me down. I was sitting at a table with a bunch of other maintenance guys all in dirty coveralls at break time. I hadn't been working there more than a week. Suddenly out of nowhere, a face shot in front of mine from over my shoulder and asked me if the silver Tacoma with the stickers and rod vault was mine. Did I fly fish? I told him it was mine, and yeah, sure I fly fished. Then he says, *"Hey, come over here for a minute, I gotta talk to you."* I figured maybe he had something he wanted to sell. Who knew?

So off to the side of the break area, he asks me what kind of fishing I do. I told him just about anything that swims. I really like going north into the Adirondacks for brookies on small streams, but smallmouths are my favorite. I barely got the last word out before he was cutting me off and giving me the fly fishing equal to the Gettysburg Address on how great of a trout fisherman he was. I couldn't get a word in, not that I tried. I was too bewildered and blindsided to even come up with anything to say. In about five minutes time, I knew where he fished, how many times a year he fished it, how many trout he caught, how many of them a year were twenty inches or better, and that he knew the river better than anyone else alive. That last bit wasn't an assumption on my part, he told me himself.

The next day, just as he promised me, he found me again and this time fired up his digital camera to show me the hundreds of photos of all the over-twenty-inch brown trout he'd caught from this specific stretch of river. I never bothered to attempt to tell him that I knew the stretch he fished. And I never attempted to tell him that I knew it was only barley two miles long and that they were all stocked. And I never bothered to mention that I could figure out that if he was catching hundreds of browns over twenty inches out of this one short stretch and fishing the same spots every time, that he was most likely just catching the same fish over and over. I never bothered to tell him any of this because he didn't want to hear me talk anyway. He wanted to hear himself.

Lucky for me, the job was in a huge production plant and it was easy to avoid him. It didn't take very long for some of the other guys to find out that I was a fly fisherman, word travels fast, and we seem to look for like-minded individuals. They'd all grin as they asked me if he'd found me yet.

The thing is, I'm sure he was a really great angler. I saw his fly box one night in the parking lot (he practically dragged me to his truck to show it to me). It was the type of organized and perfect box that would belong to someone who'd figured out the perfect pattern for a specific place and perfected perfection. I could see that much. But there was no way I was ever going fishing with him. I probably could've learned so much from him, but I'd have gotten tired of listening to how good he was before we ever got to the river.

And if you weren't dry fly fishing for trout over twenty inches, you weren't doing it right. He'd tell you that, too. Fly fishing was for trout over twenty inches. On dry flies. Period. Walleye were to be caught on spinning rods. Bass were for something else entirely different. They had nothing to do with a fly rod and were a lower form of angling all together. I just couldn't take anyone seriously that took themselves so seriously. None of it should be that serious. To me, that's the whole point. Seriously.

At some point it becomes about you and the water, and everything else just falls into place. Fish only matter when they're caught - but don't ruin a day when they're not - and life balances out for those brief times in between all other life.

I figured this out a long time ago, but it still hits me like an epiphany on a regular basis. It's pretty much the reason I string up fly rods and struggle into waders. Why I douse myself in as much deet as I can get out of a bottle of bug spray and fight through swarms of black flies and mosquitoes; why I layer up in the winter and deal with frozen toes and frozen guides; why I drive for hours and hike for miles; and why I make spur of the moment decisions to drop what I'm doing and run out back to the creek. To find that balance. I'm still amazed at how it happens after it's happened more often than not. The feeling hasn't gotten old, hasn't become normal. I haven't become complacent about it, and I don't ever take it for granted. Each time out is like a gift I never saw coming...even though it was the very thing I went looking for.

6

Fly Rods Are Not Found in The Lawn Care Dept. Take 2

It was that time of year. The time of year that you counted down every day until trout season ended, and you either hit the couple year-round catch and release waters over and over again like a broken record for a few months, or you chased something else. I'm not strictly a trout guy, but there's something about the fact of not being able to do something anymore that makes you wish you'd had more time to do it. But I digress. It was also the time of year when little critters decide to find their way indoors to stay warm for the coming season. My indoors. So as it was, I was already chasing something else before the end of trout season. Mice.

I don't have anything against mice in the greater scheme of things; they've got a right to live just as anything else does, the way I see it. But the year before, they'd gotten into the garage and ruined a few buck tails I had drying. So while I didn't have anything against them as living creatures, personally they'd offended my better nature by ruining good fly-tying materials. And this just wouldn't stand.

I was standing in an aisle at the big chain hardware store, staring at the different devices of death and destruction to all things small and furry, wondering if I should buy the *white* plastic traps or the *black* ones. I wondered which looked more inviting or less threatening, and then I thought about AR-15s and wood stocked rifles. Lead flew out of the end of both, but the AR was looked at as scarier for some reason. People call them assault rifles because they're *black,* even though they do the same thing...throw lead. I grabbed the black traps on principle. But then my eye caught these little *live* mouse traps, and I wondered why I'd want to keep them alive? Throw'em out the door and they'll only come back, and I sure as hell wasn't going to drive three miles down the road to drop off a *mouse*.

Then the thought occurred to me that if I were a bait fisherman, maybe I'd have a use for live mice. The thoughts of big pike and browns after dark entered my mind...but I'm a fly fisherman, and a catch and release fisherman at that. Maybe if I was a catch and release *bait* fisherman (no, not just the fish but the *bait too)* I could use them.

I wondered how you could tie a live mouse to a hook without hurting it so the mouse could be released later as well. *That's where the sport would lie in bait fishing*! And I can tell you right now, after getting whipped around on the end of a fly line - and then clobbered by a big brown or a northern - to be returned to dry earth afterwards and set free, I'll bet the mouse would never come back into *my* house.

My thoughts were interrupted by a woman's voice behind me talking to her husband. "Honey, what are we looking for now?" "Oh nothing." He walked around a riding lawn mower. "I'm just looking around now." I wondered just *what in the hell was he looking around at*. There weren't any fly rods to be found in the lawn care department, so I was done looking. It was time to get out of here. I'd wasted enough time *not fishing.*

After I set the gauntlet of scary looking black assault traps in the garage, it would've been a perfect time to grab the 5wt and head out back for an hour to see what I could find in the creek on such a mild October afternoon. But *nooooo.* Holly texted me during the day saying that I needed to mow the lawn. She'd taken the boys to baseball practice so I could stay and mow. How *nice* of her. I don't know if I've ever mentioned it or not, but I *hate* mowing the lawn.

I was most of the way through it when the push mower sputtered and ran out of gas. I walked around back to get the gas can and heard the water coming over the spill way through the trees and was reminded (not that I'd forgotten) that I was mowing and not fishing. This late in the year, the weather could turn at any time. Every nice day is a gift. A gift like today, and not being able to fish, was the equivalent of getting a gift card for your favorite fly shop and when you go to use it, it's expired. If I was lucky, this would be the last time I'd have to mow this year.

As I leaned over the mower pouring gas, aggravation was setting in. Such a beautiful day. Somewhere, maybe just a couple hundred yards from the house even, someone else was fishing while I cut the damn lawn. I lowered the mower deck to *scalp*. I *hoped* I'd set it low enough that this would be the last time for the year. Then my imagination took over and a scene played in my head.

There I was standing in the driveway, wearing my lucky fishing shirt (the one with Godzilla tearing down a building), and my 5wt leaning against the Jeep. I pick up the gas can and walk around the yard splashing fuel here and there, like a mob henchman about to erase an office full of incriminating evidence. My face shows determination, with a little grin of pleasure mixed in. I stand next to the Jeep, the fly rod just behind me and to the side, and I pull a pack of cigarettes from my pocket. I don't smoke, but in this instance, it looks badass as I pull a cancer stick from the pack with my lips and light it. I take a puff, and then with my middle finger and my thumb I give the cigarette a fling onto the lawn. The lawn ignites and as the flames spread I feel the heat as I turn and pick up my fly rod. "The lawn's *done*. I'm going fishing."

The cigarette thing works in the movies...

7

Wet Elk

The garage smelled like a wet elk. I didn't stutter. I live in Upstate NY, and no, we don't have any elk. I've never even had contact with an elk anywhere else, either. Yet, I can tell you now that I know what a wet elk smells like. And my garage...it smelled like wet elk.

Once you start fly fishing, your life probably changes a little bit, and there's a good chance that it changes a lot. If it doesn't, there's an even better chance that you're doing something wrong. But there's something that goes along with fly fishing that also changes your life. At least the same amount as what standing in a river sending loops out over the water on a quiet summer morning does for you. Only it's probably not a change in the same direction or with the same life organizing and prioritizing qualities that the actual act of learning to love the cast of a fly rod can bring to you. No. This fly-tying stuff that can turn an organized and neatly arranged life - just like the tying bench and all flat surfaces within a twenty-foot radius - into mass chaos. Or in the least, a cluttered heap of feathers and fur, the likes of which you couldn't even find at a zoo.

Some anglers manage to avoid it somehow, while some of us act as though we may be a little better, more connected to fly fishing because of it. But secretly we might envy the ones who don't participate in the practice. It has its good points and not so good points as well. I suppose everything does.

When I started tying, I began with nothing but a few different colors of marabou and some black hackles. I was actually tying jigs, still fishing with a spinning rod, but tying jigs was the gateway drug into fly fishing and fly *tying*. Once you start *tying* you never look at anything the same again. And more importantly, you're *always* looking. And your friends and family know it, too.

A couple years ago, I thought it would be cool to start obtaining tying materials from places other than in bags on a rack at a store. So I put the word out to a couple friends that if they shot a pheasant during hunting season, I'd clean it and skin it for them if I could have the cape. I got a text a week later that read, *I left you a surprise out back where the dog can't reach them.* I remember thinking to myself, "*them?*" When I got home I found five pheasants, de-breasted and waiting to be caped out. Five birds, three males and two females. I now have enough pheasant in my storage drawers to last me the next four-hundred and twenty-four years, give or take.

Not long after that, another friend, Pat Lasher, who both hunts and cleans and butchers deer for other people, asked if I wanted any buck tails. Well of course I said sure I did. I had grand plans of dying some crazy colors for streamers, and by the end of the season I had about a dozen. I de-boned them and used my tool box in the back of my truck as a drying space so that I wouldn't have to answer to my wife for the garage smelling like dead animals. Coincidentally, I'd used the same box to dry the pheasant capes in the back yard, too. It worked great…kept the bugs and mice away and the garage didn't stink.

It's funny some of the questions you start getting from people once they find out you tie flies and that you get stuff from wherever you can. The morning my wife called me from work to tell me there was a deer on the side of the road with a big bushy tail, I knew she'd given in to the fact that this was happening and there was nothing she could do but accept it. Naturally, I told her it was illegal for me to just pull to the shoulder and start hacking parts off a dead deer, but I appreciated the fact that she'd not only accepted it but was *actually looking* for me, too.

Then there are the conversations that come out of nowhere. The ones you didn't think you'd ever have, and that the friend or family member that started it never saw coming. They may become a little bewildered by your knowledge of such things, even. *"Hey, there's a dead blue jay outside my bedroom window. It must have flown into the glass. Do you want it for tying flies?"* When you answer them politely, *"Thanks, but no, it's illegal to possess song birds or their feathers because they're federally protected."* You get that shocked, *"Oh, I didn't know that...how do you know so much about them?"* It becomes comical eventually.

You can only explain to so many people that you've been offered dead birds that flew into windows so many times, that it's simply good knowledge to have and it comes with the territory. Of course, if you're constantly offered dead things - road kill and birds that fly into windows - you're either in a very economically depressed part of the world where such things are probably as normal as our run to the grocery store, or you tie your own flies and the people around you find it somewhat fascinating. Fascinating enough to even think to offer you a dead blue jay in the first place. As a matter of fact, I doubt there are many other people, besides fly fisherman, who get offered dead blue jays. We're kind of in a separate category from the rest of society when it comes to some things, I guess.

I got a text from Pat Lasher once, the one who got me all the buck tails. He had a friend who was a taxidermist and the question was simple and straight forward enough. *"I got a bunch of different deer, elk, bear, sheep, and coyote. It's all tanned. Do you want it?"* Once again, the obvious answer was *yes.* I was picturing a bag of little scraps that would've been left from the taxidermist work creating trophy mounts. Small scraps.

The next day, I got home and two bags - one plastic grocery bag and one tall bag about the size of a pillowcase - were outside the front door. They were full of *large* scraps, ten times the size I was expecting. Jake had seen it and called Holly. I'm sure the conversation would have sounded a bit *odd* to anyone overhearing them, but it probably seemed pretty normal to my wife and son.

He told her there were a bunch of animal furs outside the door when he got home, and she told him to just leave them there for me to bring in later. The problem was they were moved from the doorway so Jake could get in, and when I got home, the grocery bag had been just out far enough to get wet from the sloppy snow falling. So an old broken slatted headboard in the garage that I'd failed to throw out made for the perfect drying rack. Procrastination does pay off sometimes, even if in the oddest ways.

The next morning the question was asked, *"What's that smell in the garage?"* It was a simple answer, straightforward, and in most other houses in the area would have gotten a raised eyebrow and more thorough questions. In my house, the answer fails to warrant even the batting of an eye. *"It's just wet elk."*

8

Hail Mary Casts

I wasn't exactly positive why I was out there. I mean, I knew why I loaded the canoe on the Jeep in the wind and pitch dark the night before, and I knew why I drove there straight from work. But I didn't know *why*, since I didn't expect to catch anything. Time was limited this late in the year.

After work I only had about two hours of light left before the stars started to glimmer in the cold fall sky. Or, like on that day, before the clouds stole away another twenty minutes by snuffing out the twilight that much earlier. I loaded up the canoe in the dark the night before because it was the only time I could finally get out there to do it. And I was there on the water now because it was the only light left and the closest water I could get to in a hurry. But like I said, I didn't figure on catching anything, so…why?

The 7wt was rigged up with a full sinking line, a 30lb mono leader and twelve inches of wire connected to a five-inch streamer. Buck tail, flash, eyes and UV resin…I had tied it the night before, literally right before loading up the canoe for no other reason than I hadn't tied anything in a couple weeks, at least. The tying bench had been a pile of chaos for just as long easily, and I told myself if I tied something I'd need to clean the bench up first. So maybe it was just the motivation to clean that I needed. So I did.

I picked everything up, placed hackles back into bags, picked up two buck tails, sorted some marabou I'd tossed into a pile like the neighbor's leaves out to the curb, vacuumed feathers and hair and hung bobbins. And then I got back out a pack of hooks, a bag of strung hackles, two more buck tails, and a bundle of flash and proceeded to lay the cleaned and orderly tying bench to waste in a matter of minutes. Nothing lasts forever.

It was getting cold. Not the day, but the time of year. It didn't get much above forty that day, and now it was in the upper thirties as the sun hid behind the gray clouds and dropped closer to the horizon. I made a few casts to what I believed was deep water on the edge of a drop off, but who knew for sure. I was just guessing by the fact that the weeds had stopped, and that I could let the sinking line pull the streamer down quite a ways and I still wasn't hitting the bottom.

I was making slow retrieves, but every now and then I'd give a quick short shake to add a little frantic jerk to what I felt looked like a good bait fish imitation. But for all I knew there were two pike down there swimming alongside it laughing their asses off, nudging each other now and then with tears of laughter in their eyes and motioning up to me with a head movement. Fish making jokes at my expense. Sounded reasonable.

On the trail that paralleled the canal, a mountain bike went by. A wave from a gloved rider with a big winter jacket, a beanie hat, and his breath in the air. Quick short puffs. They were probably Indian smoke signals for *hey stupid, it's cold out and you're standing out there in a canoe in the wind casting to nothing.* It could've been worse. I'd forgotten gloves and it could've been snowing. My fingers weren't as cold as they could've been.

The onset of fall, knowing winter was right behind it, sent me into a bit of a panic. It was like suddenly getting slapped in the face with a black leather glove full of reality. The reality that time does indeed run out for everyone sooner or later. It comes sooner for those of us in the north where the snow and ice could at any time cover our opportunities - many of them, anyhow - for months. It sent me into a bit of a panic. One that had me in a canoe on a cold day after work making Hail Mary casts to fish that may or may not have been there. I figured if nothing else, there was probably some kind of story in it somewhere if I looked hard enough.

9

Steelhead

Winters in Upstate N.Y. are probably like winters any place that get really cold and snowy. I won't be that guy that goes on and on about how bad our winters are here. How cold they can get. How much snow we can get. For every population that thinks they have it tougher than everyone else, there's usually another town or city somewhere that can claim to have it worse. About the only thing I'm confident stating that we have more of than anyone else is taxes. I imagine soon they'll be taxing snowflakes up here somehow, then we'll actually have a reason to complain about it snowing.

But as far as winters go, I usually welcome whatever the new season on its way in may be, simply because as much as I fear change the older I get, a change of season is normally a nice change. If at least in the very beginning, before it's been around just long enough to start complaining about it again like each previous year.

At first, the new season is almost welcomed, if for nothing else because it's a change. Fall is beautiful in the beginning, with all the leaves turning bright reds and oranges and purples; but after the leaves have fallen, you're left with a bunch of gray, except for the pines. And the pines, when surrounded by gray and less sunlight, lose their rich green somehow. It might be a mental thing just because of all the gray, but the evergreens seem to lose most of their luster surrounded by so much...*blah*.

But after the snow has been around long enough, the new season wears off and you're ready for another change. Except you're *really* ready for it. So much so that you begin to dwell on it. And depending on how early the first snow might fall, like say as early as October, and how late the snow might stay, like say April, that can become a long period of dread. *"They"* say that the winter has the highest percentage of suicides, and I have to believe that it has a lot to do with the lack of colors, and if you're an angler...*fishing.*

I'd always avoided the Salmon River up in Pulaski because if I wanted to go to the circus I'd buy tickets and enjoy a bag of peanuts while I sat under the Big Top. Every year I'd have friends and anglers who I'd just met alike, inviting me up to go steelheading and every year I'd decline all the same. It's just not my *idea* of what the *idea is,* which is to *get away*. Get away from other people, and just *get away* from it all in general.

But the winter of 2016 was my breaking point for a couple reasons. One was the winter itself. We finally had a good dependable snow fall, one where you pretty much knew that you needed to get up early the next morning to clean off the vehicles and shovel or snow blow. The past few winters had been hit or miss; maybe it would snow, maybe not. But this winter was like the winters I remembered as a kid, which told me two things...I was *getting older*, and I was *feeling* like I was getting older. I was beginning to sound like all the *older people* who were around when I *was* younger. *It was always worse when you were younger.*

The other reason was that I just couldn't take what a real winter meant anymore. Frozen lakes and three feet of snow along the creeks were not my idea of a relaxing day on the water. I'd had enough.

Early in the season, I'd met a friend, Josh Kelly, out on the ice on Lake Delta for something a little different. It was actually a really nice day. A light wind that died down to almost perfectly still a few times, a bright blue sky, and venison on the grill with a cold beer never killed anyone...that I know, anyway. Of course, one beer these days might *feel* like it's trying to kill me. Just adds to the feeling old part. So, all in all, it was a really good day. I didn't do any fishing myself, I just went to hang out with a friend and talk fishing and life.

I followed Josh back and forth and watched him pull a few pickerel and perch through the ice, but it wasn't something I've ever longed to go out and do every weekend during the winter. I'm just more of a moving-water type of guy. Not a move-the-water-around-in-the-hole-so-it-doesn't-freeze kind of guy.

At some point, social media being what it is, someone offered me a spare bedroom and a tour of a couple of their favorite waters out in Buffalo. The kid's name was Justin, and there I was feeling old again as I realized I was calling someone probably in their thirties *a kid*. He told me we could go chase just about anything from trout to smallmouths to musky or steelhead, and that they didn't have all the snow over there that we had three hours east.

Holly wanted to know how I knew this guy wasn't an ax murderer, and I told her I didn't. But he had some good fishy shots on his page, and if he did turn out to be an ax murderer...well, the story could be even better than originally expected. What did I have to lose? Besides my head in a refrigerator, maybe.

I planned to make the three-hour drive on a Thursday after work, giving us Friday through Sunday to chase fish. So on a Wednesday evening, I loaded up the Jeep. The fishing out by Buffalo was pretty wide open as far as winter fly fishing goes, so I was packing every rod I owned to cover everything. Around home, I had the Oriskany Creek out my back door that was open to catch and release browns all winter, a two-mile section on the

West Canada Creek called the Trophy Section that was the same, and then the Salmon River that I tried to avoid.

I actually *did* fish the Salmon River in January - just once - for about an hour, but conditions were *less than favorable*, to say the least. We'd set up a fly-tying day at the Tailwater Lodge, JP and I, and the lodge had given us room deals. This meant we stayed a night, fished the next morning, then set up our vices in their tasting room where there was a mile-long list of beers on tap to *"sample"* while we sat around and tied flies and told stories.

Just some random information here. Samples are very small beers, but when you drink enough of them, they feel like they're trying to kill me all the same. Ulcers don't like samples as much as they don't like full beers.

Four of us hit the river at 7am. Myself, Wayne Weber, Charlie Warfield, and Frank Geremski. It was a balmy thirteen degrees on the upside of the zero, and I believe it was the coldest temperature I'd ever fished, or at least *attempted* to fish in. Wayne's a guide on the river, and not only is the schoolhouse pool right behind the lodge, but Wayne fishes it and puts clients on it all the time. So I wasn't surprised to see the one and only steelhead of the morning on *his* line.

My line, on the other hand, didn't see anything but ice. Let me tell you that thirteen degrees doesn't mean a whole lot more than everything is frozen. And what isn't frozen is in the process of freezing.

I was casting my 7wt with a heavy nymph pattern, cleaning ice out of the guides about every two casts, while watching Wayne standing in the river with his left hand inside his wader's chest pocket and his right simply roll casting up current and repeating when the drift downstream was complete. In the crotch of his left arm rested against his chest was a hot plastic mug of coffee. He looked comfortable, as comfortable as a person standing in a river while it was thirteen degrees could look, anyway. While I struggled with the nuances of casting lines and leaders that would freeze stiff because I was too slow at getting them back in the water.

The last time I tried to cast, the leader had frozen solid and moved more like a wire than a leader. And when it wrapped itself around the tip section of the rod, it ended up a frozen mess of line and rod that I no longer had the want, or finger dexterity, to deal with. I exited the river stage right and watched Wayne and Frank fish, while Charlie and I discussed a possible day on the West Canada soon while listening to my neoprene waders freeze solid.

A little while later, inside at breakfast, everyone sat relatively quiet while they ate, and Wayne asked me if I planned on going back out. I told him I wasn't going to be the guy to call the game on account of the cold, but I sure as hell wasn't going to be the first one to lead the way. If I saw someone else headed back out, I'd follow their lead. No one ever went back out.

Later while we tied flies and drank, Brian Benner, the Tailwater's sales manager, was hanging out with us and asked me if the stories in my book were all true. I told him no one would make up stories about catching little fish or getting skunked. He replied with *fair enough*. I'm still not sure what he was really thinking. Somehow that was all still a good weekend; I suppose frostbite is a sting, and all stings fade away over time.

So...Buffalo. I loaded up the Jeep with every rod I owned, with a stack of fly boxes with everything from nymphs to dries to streamers, with neoprene waders and my lighter weight Simms. Boots, a couple different nets, and a sleeping bag and a backpack with a couple changes of clothes. It was probably almost everything I owned. Holly asked me if I wanted to take her car, of course after the Jeep was loaded, and my initial thought was *of course not. This is a fishing trip.*

No self-respecting fisherman would go on a fishing trip with his wife's SUV when he has a lifted Jeep Cherokee with a roof rack and rod vault on the top and a winch. It was a three-hour drive and there was no telling if the winch might come in handy on that trip down the highway, and come on…it's a fishing trip. You have to take the Jeep.

But then she brought up the gas mileage, and I thought about that. And then she mentioned the heated seats, and how nice they'd be after standing in cold winter rivers all day long. I swapped everything into her car and dropped my Jeep keys into her purse. She was right, but I wouldn't have admitted to these things on my own, because…well, lifted Jeeps.

The drive out to Buffalo from Utica takes about three hours, and it's nothing but long, straight, and boring. It gives you nothing but time to think, and the whole reason I go fishing is so I don't have to think. So, if some people will tell you half the fun is getting there, then I'll just add that sometimes it's only a necessary evil. Holly's new Mitsubishi SUV rode smoothly. I'd ridden in it a hundred times before, but on a road trip like this - all alone and left to my own thoughts and observations - that smooth ride started me thinking.

It was *too* smooth. The Jeep had rattles and squeaks, it was seventeen years old after all, but it probably had some of them even when it was new. Leaf springs and straight axles just don't ride smooth, but you don't realize how rough they ride until you get completely used to it and then jump into something smooth and spend a long, lonely and quiet ride in it. I scanned the radio stations since her car doesn't have a cassette player, yet another thing that I loved about the Cherokee. I couldn't find anything worth listening to most of the ride, and when I did finally pick up a station playing Judas Priest, it just felt all wrong cranking it up in such a clean, quiet, and smooth car. Her car made me feel *old*.

And that's when it hit me. The Jeep wasn't so much about being my fish mobile to Batman's Batmobile, it was more about making me feel *young*.

It reminded me of all the old trucks I had when I was a young airman in Florida. The Jeep rode rough. It squeaked and rattled, it got bad gas mileage. I could still plug in the same old AC/DC tapes that I listened to in those old trucks in the Jeep. It had its little mechanical quirks, like the passenger door latch that stuck and the sagging headliner. And then there was the lift kit and the winch, neither of which I actually needed. Driving in the wife's car, I felt old. Responsible. Boring. In the Jeep I felt younger. Holly hated the Jeep. I loved it.

I snapped to and realized I was two exits from Buffalo. The highway in front of me was a long string of red taillights, the sky looked like a tie-died t-shirt as the sun dropped below the horizon.

Finding Justin's house was easier than I'd been afraid it would be, if only because I don't like - or do well - driving in city traffic. Especially when I'm in an unfamiliar place. I parked in front of a small brick house in a questionable neighborhood; only questionable because I didn't know it and there were no picket fences. I hit the lock button on the key fob twice, just to be sure.

I'm sure it wasn't a bad neighborhood at all, but it wasn't my little town, and not out in the country; so to me it may as well have been the setting for the plot of one of those big city cop TV shows where they find some poor bastard who was just in town to go fishing dead in an alley and they spend the next sixty minutes chasing leads to find out his wife was having an affair with his dentist and she never meant for this to happen.

It was almost 10pm when I walked into the house, greeted by Justin and his beagle, Earl. While I was sure Justin and I would get along just fine being a couple fly guys, it was apparent after patting Earl on the head that Earl believed we were going to be best buddies. He was bringing me toys to throw almost immediately. Dogs are friendlier than most humans deserve, in all reality.

Justin's place was fairly plain. Hardwood floor, no carpet, a couch and a coffee table and flat screen in the living room, and that was about it. Looking around, the couch, coffee table and TV were the only amenities besides the kitchen table and beds in the bedrooms that didn't have something to do with fly fishing. The décor was scarce, to say the least. You might even think, at first glance, that he was either just moving in or just moving out, the walls were so bare.

What wasn't necessary furniture was necessary fly fishing and that was about it. Waders hung from the curtain rod in the front window, a couple fly boxes and reels rested on a pile of jackets and clothes. The only other thing in the living room was a rope toy that Earl had shredded into a million little strings, covering everything from the floor to the couch everywhere. I got the feeling it had been there for a while by the obvious somewhat clear path through it on the floor as we walked out to the kitchen.

The kitchen, as it was, was even barer than the rest of the house. A trash can, a fridge, and a table with two chairs. I caught sight of the empty popcorn machine on top of the fridge covered in fly fishing decals, but before I could consider its oddness in an otherwise empty house, my eyes turned to the table. It was covered in fly boxes full of streamers. And where there were no fly boxes full of streamers, there were just piles of streamers...some big and some huge, the length of my forearm or more. The whole table looked like some type of Jim Henson nightmare. Enough feathers and fur and huge hooks to send any

PETA activist into full-on convulsions. I removed fly boxes from one of the chairs and we sat down and talked. I half expected to be offered a beer, which I would have had to turn down because they try to kill me, but later in the evening I got a glimpse inside the fridge, and it was practically empty. A couple take out boxes and a case of water.

As we talked, I was trying to take it all in - that there was nothing in his house but fly-fishing stuff - while thinking about my own house full of family pictures, books on shelves, plants, kid's toys, bills stacked on the kitchen counter...what I'd come to consider *normal*. The thing was, though, as we sat and talked over that table piled with musky streamers, I realized that if I was single, if there was no wife and kids back home, I wasn't sure my place would be much different at all. Ok, I'd still have a bookshelf full of every book I came across that had anything to do with fishing, but even those would still count as nothing in the house *except fishing stuff*.

I'm not saying I was envious of his current situation of appearing like a broke fish bum, but I'm not saying I didn't feel a little bit jealous of it either. My eyes fell back up to the popcorn machine with the fly-fishing stickers on it a few times. There was nothing in the house; everything was minimal, to say the least. It seemed to be the only thing that wasn't minimal and decided the only reason it made sense at all was because of the stickers.

I slept in a spare bedroom with nothing but a single bed and a desk covered in the remnants of flies tied in the past, which seemed to also be all over the bed, along with Earl's white hair. Like I said, I wasn't envious of his state of living, but I couldn't say I'd be much different left on my own, either. I knew that given the chance, I'd put everything into fly fishing and nothing into anything else. So yes, I *was* slightly jealous.

The next morning, we were on the road at five-thirty and after a twenty-minute drive we were sliding down a steep bank to a river. It didn't look all that different here at dawn by the bridge we'd parked at than my home creek. Back home, the stones would be mostly smooth and round cobblestones, but here they were more smooth and flat, with varied colors all the same. The water wasn't more than knee deep, but it was just a long and straight shallow run.

Then as the light in the sky started to grow, so did the details. The biggest difference from the creeks back home was the tint of light green the water had when there was a little depth, not much past a couple feet. I found it intriguing, that it didn't look *dirty*, just green. Kind of like watered-down mint, if that makes any sense at all.

The first hole we came to was around the first bend, and we set our gear down on the inside bank, a wide and bare dry creek bottom of sun-bleached river stones. In the hole rested a naked tree, a huge thing devoid of all bark that laid in the hole length wise, like a person sprawling out on a couch to take up all the room. I put my 7wt together and Justin went into guide mode. He was rigging up his rod to Czech nymph and asked if I'd ever done it. I told him no, I was a streamer guy, and he asked me bluntly if I wanted to catch a steelhead or not.

He was going to rig my 7wt up with a Czech nymph rig, but as soon as he had it in his hand, I could see the look on his face. *"I gotta cast this thing, is that cool?"* I told him of course. He made a few casts then hooked the streamer in the hook keeper. *"I can't put a Czech nymph rig on this thing. It's got way too much soul."* I understood what he meant about the soul, but didn't understand *why* he meant it, basically because I'd never Czech nymphed.

He showed me what to do then handed me his fly rod, a rod with mush less *soul,* and after my first flip of the line with a bead, a hook, and some split shot, I understood. Czech nymphing was fly fishing only in the sense that you used a fly rod, but you could really do the same thing with a long spinning rod. He was adamant that this was how I was going to catch a steelhead on this day, and that it had to be a bead, this color, and not a nymph. So I figured I'd driven three hours and slept on a bed covered in dog fur for nothing more than a chance, and if I had the chance to catch a steelhead, I should probably take the best chance I could get. So I rolled with it.

Now there's not a whole lot that will make me feel like an idiot when it comes to fly fishing, simply because I'm not very good at any of it to begin with. So to me, being not so good, or marginal at best at just about any of it, it all feels fairly normal to be *not very good at it* and still have a good time. When I find something that I'm *really not good at* with a fly rod, I *really* feel like an idiot. And for the first half hour or so that's how Czech nymphing made me feel.

I couldn't get the drift, or more accurately the drag of the rig on the bottom, ticking along feeling every little rock and piece of gravel like I thought I should, and it was only a matter of about five minutes drifting the same fifteen feet along that submerged tree that I missed my first steel head. I felt the tension - the fish had it - and it took off up the hole and under the opposite side of the tree trunk. Before I ever thought to set the hook good and solid, it was gone. I laughed, shook my head, and dredged the spot a few more times. Justin kept telling me there were more fish there, there were more; but I was only picturing the pale bead in my head, bouncing the bottom past nothing.

He took the rod from me and showed me just where to drop the rig in, how to drag it along the bottom at just the right speed, how to keep it just under the tree's entire length, and then…bam. The rod doubled over, and he pulled back with everything he had.

The line cut the water and the fish first went up stream under the tree and then turned back down like a formula one race car at full speed in a hairpin turn. It shot downstream, upstream and downstream both being under this brown and smooth naked tree carcass in a hole no more than twenty-five feet long, and I couldn't help but think there was no way this fish was coming out of this hole. Every factor, which was mostly the tree and the couple large limbs still attached and hidden in the mint green tinted water, was in the fish's favor.

At what I thought was the end of the fight, the fish shot under the tree to the far side where it seemed to anchor itself in place. Justin pulled back, the rod mimicked the St. Louis Arch, and nothing happened. I figured the leader was wrapped around limbs that couldn't be seen, but I pictured a steelhead resting in an easy chair with a magazine and a cigar while the leader was tied in a perfect bow around a branch. I still see things as cartoons in my head like when I was a child; in the least it adds humor to times when I could do nothing better than panic or swear and yell. Then it took off again, but this time it was only a few tugs back and forth before I was netting it in the shallows.

Justin felt horrible because he'd taken the rod to show me how to do it and then caught the fish, but I thought it was as cool as anything else I'd ever seen in the past that I'd labeled *cool*; maybe even cooler than most. He tried to correct a mistake I was making once more in the same hole under the same tree and hooked into another but didn't land it and felt just as bad again. I had to remind him that I didn't make the trip for him to guide me so I could catch my first steelhead. I'd just come to fish. And we were fishing, so it was all good. We moved on downstream.

It was full on daylight now, so my initial assessment in the early hints of daylight that this creek wasn't much different than the ones back home was quickly recognized in my head as extremely off point. Dead wrong. Where we'd come down a steep incline through the woods by the bridge in the dark, that incline was now gone and instead there were shear walls of rock. The rock ran in horizontal lines, layers of shale in hues of gray through dull blues and reds. It was something of a spectacle and I found myself looking around at the small canyon we were in as much as I was looking for my next place to try and dredge up a steelhead.

With the walls closing in, and the river narrowing between them, the depth was a more constant knee to waist-deep, and with the depth came a more solid mint tint to the water. Where I was used to the dark tea stained waters in the Adirondacks, the ones where sunlight showed the depths as a dark red with hints of shapes of rocks and deadfalls, here the water was simply light green. There was no seeing anything a couple feet down no matter how hard I looked. It was a place like this where it truly paid off to know how to read water. Justin obviously knew the river, but I also knew he was reading the water too, because he was just that good. Me? I was just dropping it in along boulders and seams, hoping for the best. But it was easy to hope for the best in such a beautiful place.

There were these crazy rocks that were the size of a small kitchen table scattered along this stretch of river that became a moment of enlightenment for me. Shaped like what most people think of when they hear *UFO,* I was trying to place in my head where I'd seen rocks just like these before when it finally hit me.

Some years earlier while working on the road climbing cell towers, while the other guys on the crews I worked on usually found a bar each night, I'd find a place to fish. One of my favorite but most unusual places to fish was the Owasco River, straight through the middle of the small city of Auburn. The Owasco River flowed out of Owasco Lake, one of the Finger Lakes, but I didn't fish it where it was wide and deep outside of town. I'd spotted it while on top of the cell tower that we always worked on in town almost directly below, just across the street. I fished the section that was a small stream on the bottom side of a little dam, a section that was littered with broken glass and bricks from most likely old factories that once stood along the stream and, well, litter. Lots of litter. Did I mention it went right through the middle of town?

Anyway, these same rocks were all along the tiny Owasco as it flowed through a tiny wooded area in between the main highway cutting through the city and a smaller neighborhood street, and I'd always thought with all the glass and bricks in the river from old industrial buildings, that they must have been some type of old factory tooling. They all looked the same, more or less, and were more or less the same size and color. I'd used them as stepping stones and casting perches a hundred times probably, and only guessed at their originations.

Justin called them *concretions,* and at first I thought he was just making up a name or calling them by something he'd just heard other people call them by. I'd never heard of such a thing before and hell, I had a pretty damn impressive rock collection back in grade school, if I do say so myself. Concretion? Yeah, that must be some name some fishermen made up. Of course, later on after the trip I'd Google the stupid name and find out for the thousandth time in my life that I'm just not as smart as I sometimes think I am, because concretion was indeed the actual name. I claim to be a diehard fly fisherman. I never claimed to be smart.

It was about twenty feet upstream of one of the biggest *concretions* I'd seen where I finally hooked into steel. And I don't mean a piece of rebar from an old derelict bridge upstream somewhere. It was a textbook holding pool, something more like what I'd expect to fish for smallmouth or possibly browns. The pool wasn't much bigger than my Jeep Cherokee, really; it may have been more of the size of a two-door where mine was a four-door. Now that I think about it, I'm not sure if the two-door is any shorter than a four-door or if they just put longer doors on the two-door models. It doesn't really matter unless you're the type of person to claim to know your Jeeps, which I'm not. I just drive the thing. I'd just as easily drive a pick-up or a station wagon if it would get me to the fish. The proof of that was that my wife's Mitsubishi was parked back by the bridge where we started. Not my Jeep.

It was a small pool, flanked on the far side by the shear shale wall with one lone tree growing out of the base just above the waterline, and on the near side it was outlined by several boulders. I stood along the edge of the boulders and made a half-ass cast - more of a flip because that's what you do when Czech nymphing - into the head of the pool where water was washing over a shelf of rock.

It all happened so fast, but I know Justin said something behind me about getting ready because I was about to find a fish, and I was going about it all cool and calm like it was just another walk on a river, when all hell broke loose.

I found myself trying to stop a fish that wasn't stopping for me. It was stopping and changing directions more because of the size of the pool and where the boulders were telling it to go. It definitely wasn't listening to *my directions*. Justin was trying to coach me, but whatever he was saying off to the side was just excited white noise in my ears. I was holding onto the Saint Louis Arch doing my best to finish an eight second ride, and the steel head was doing its best to buck me off.

When it was all said and done - quicker than it seems in my memory now, I'm sure - Justin got the fish in the net and my adrenaline slowly curbed itself. It was the largest and certainly most powerful fish I'd ever had on a fly rod, and I'd always sworn that the smallmouth bass was the strongest freshwater fish we had. That's still a debate in my head, but I'll say this much...steelhead have a reputation due to what they can actually do, not simply because fishermen tell stories. Let's get this straight...fishermen tell stories *because of fish like the steelhead.*

The rest of the day was spent moving downstream and searching but not finding any more. The lack of fish lead to conversations more about life than fishing, which is one of those things that happens when you're on a river naturally. Justin's fish bum lifestyle began to make more sense as I learned more about him, and I found myself not so jealous anymore about the apartment with the rudimentary living room furniture and kitchen table piled with musky streamers and not much else.

Not too long ago he'd been engaged, but it had fallen through before the wedding ever took place. He'd lost everything. I could tell by the way he talked that when he lost everything, he didn't mean a house and the things that fill it. He mentioned the house, but it wasn't what he lost. He meant any semblance of happiness. He lost everything, namely himself.

He seemed like a guy on the downhill side now, making his way back to the world, but the uphill battle had taken a toll on him. I could tell. I was suddenly thinking of my family back home, the problems Holly and I had gone through and gotten past in our marriage, my boys. As all things usually do when you spend enough time on a river, life came in to perspective for me.

The next morning was Sunday, and plans were loose at best. But when you're talking about fishing, loose plans are full of hope and expectations at worst. The ever-present and world-bonding

Facebook came through once again, and it was set up that we'd meet Anthony Horton somewhere east of Buffalo. The plan was to meet and fish for a while and then at an undetermined time, basically when the fishing was done or I felt like going home, I'd take off back to the NYS Thruway and head east.

I followed Justin's taillights in the pre-daylight darkness for only maybe twenty minutes before we came upon some taillights parked on the side of the road just off a bridge. When I met Tony for the first time, he was in waders. And if first impressions are everything, the waders - combined with a bubbling smile through a beard of black and gray - are the first impression you wish everyone you met would make; or in the least, the one you wish you could make yourself. Tony is that one guy that you instantly like in the first initial few seconds, for no other reason than you don't see any reason *not to like him*. I only knew him from a couple of fly-fishing pages on Facebook, that cold and heartless internet thing.

Whichever river was flowing under the bridge I don't remember, but Tony said that it had rained overnight, and the water had risen and was colored up. A flashlight down over the railing confirmed it, so I looked at the two locals and waited for the next idea.

Oak Orchard was that one place that I'd heard of but never fished for two reasons. One, it was at least three hours from home and there were closer places to catch trout. Two, it was synonymous with tales that equaled or rivalled the stories of the Salmon River where close quarters combat fishing was the norm. And if I could get to the Salmon River in just under an hour and hadn't bothered during the big season, I sure wasn't going to drive more than three for more of the same. I shuddered when I heard them discussing *The Oak,* but I also made the drive out for the weekend to fish places I'd never fished with people I'd never fished with, and here I was two for two. I followed them to Oak

Orchard, trying to prepare myself for the worst while hoping for, well...something less than the worst.

It wasn't exactly shoulder-to-shoulder everywhere, but in a few places it was. Tony and Justin stood back and surveyed the situation. They laughed, pointing out the guy standing in the river up to the bottom of his wader's chest pocket, both agreeing that he was probably practically standing on fish and casting out to nothing. If he'd stood on the bank and stayed dry and made a six-foot cast, he may have had a chance at hooking up. There was more of the same up and down river. I guess you'll have a lot of that in the places that are just too easy to get to for pretty much everyone.

We worked our way upstream and took a spot across the river from some guys fishing center pin gear. I'd never done it, but I knew that anyone who fly fished was automatically expected to unconditionally hate it. It looked to me that they were doing the same thing as everyone else, just drifting something, hoping for something to happen. I couldn't muster up any hate.

We had a super steep wooded incline to our backs, so casting any distance with my 7wt was a challenge, to say the least. And this was where I got my first real world experience with spey rods. Tony was fishing an old glass spey rod, and it was one of the coolest things I'd ever seen since picking up fly fishing. It looked so easy. He made it look easy.

We were staying spread out. The idea was we'd all make a cast, let it swing, then step down river three steps and repeat the swing again. At the bottom of our run, the first person would return to the top and we'd continue covering that short piece of water foot by foot. Plus, that would keep anyone from creeping in and crowding us. It wasn't really *hogging* the river for ourselves, it was just taking up enough of it that hopefully no one else would try to horn in on it. Tony had the best rod for the job, hands down.

He offered the spey rod up to me to give it a shot, and after a little prodding I accepted. I felt sloppy at first, like anything tried for the first time, but it didn't take long before I had the hang of it enough to clumsily cover almost the entire width of the river. In the same place with my single handed 7wt, I was having a hard time making it halfway across. I was dreaming up ways to add another rod to my arsenal...like I needed anymore dreams.

I didn't hook a fish at Oak Orchard, but Tony did...a nice rainbow that was just small enough that he didn't call it a steelhead. But it was still a really nice trout that anyone would've been happy to net. And Justin did the honors on the net end. It was only one of three fish we saw hooked at all out of about a hundred or more anglers. I'm not saying the fish weren't there - not at all. I'm just saying that some days the odds are in the fish's favor if for no other reason than we're only human.

10

Brook Trout

In 2011, JP founded this thing called Trout Power. It's a cool story in itself, but it's a story that deserves its own place on a bookshelf, so I'll run down the short version for now...and how it led to me catching the biggest small-stream brook trout of my life.

In 2011, he founded Trout Power under his rod company, JP Ross Fly Rods. The idea behind it was that one of our biggest local trout rivers - a river the state touted as one of the most renowned trout streams in central New York - had its flows controlled by several impoundments, and there were always questions on what the erratic flows meant to the ecosystem.

JP knew that there was no better gauge for a river ecosystem than trout. He was a fly fisherman after all, and that kind of thing just seems common knowledge to people like us. If only it were to everyone *else*. Sure, plenty of people love to gossip and theorize, but JP is that guy who'll always ask you to *prove it;* and when no one can or will - when it comes to certain things, like wild trout - he's the one to step up and actually act.

His idea was to start this *Trout Power* thing, make it a tournament/creel study, and use it to collect data to get some hard facts or at least some sound theories on what the crazy up and down shoot from the hip surges from the dams meant to the ecosystem in the river.

After two years and two catch and release tournaments, he had the evidence that he was looking for. There were no fish larger than your standard stocked-sized fish in the river except for the trophy section where catch and release was the rule year-round. There you'll find the big fish - holdovers, released breeders, the bigger browns. But still nothing small enough to say there was any natural reproduction going on in the West Canada Creek. No one caught any fingerlings, nothing under eight inches, except for in the tributaries where they were known to hold wild fish; tribs were actually designated as wild fish streams by the state.

He used money from the tournaments to sink temperature sensors up and down the river in the deep holes, and he even used the third year to promote not a tournament, but a stream cleanup day. He probably learned just as much that third year as the first two because no one except his friends, the Smith family, showed up. They walked the stream and collected garbage bags full of trash left behind by both anglers and tubers alike, but since there was no fishing that day and no prizes, the support was gone.

It's also funny to realize that during those first two tournament years, I heard anglers all over our area constantly ranting whenever Trout Power came up in a conversation at the local big box outdoors stores, them saying that JP was only doing it to sell fly rods. I'd bring up the fact that Patagonia used its branding to make money that it donated to conservation, so why wouldn't it count when someone local with a successful business did the same?

It boggled my mind, but it's always been my experience that people - no matter what it is they're into (custom cars, fishing, woodworking, needlepoint, etc.) - they never believe that anyone local can make a difference. And when someone does, they put them down and dismiss it because their small minds can't fathom *themselves* making a difference...so how could someone else in town ever do anything good? They'd show up to fish but were nowhere to be seen when it was time to clean things up. Hypocrites are everywhere. A small band of us saw JP for who he really was - someone not caring what others thought and trying to make a difference - so we've stood up with him since day one.

Cutting to the chase; Trout Power ended up becoming a non-profit, separating itself from his rod company, with a small board of directors who felt the same as JP, and a loyal following of anglers who realize that even your *average, nobody special, Joe Blow angler* can actually take the time to do something worthwhile and make things happen. Not just talk about it.

In 2016, we were all gathered at a lodge in the Adirondacks, about twenty-five anglers in total...all volunteers. We were there to study a stream, or more precisely, study the brook trout in the stream. The brain child once again of JP, because when he finds something that no one can explain, his whole *prove it* mentality kicks in. So we were fly fishing this small stream, collecting DNA samples from the brookies we caught, and mapping out where they were in the small watershed.

Acid rain had left this stream all but barren over twenty years ago. In the '80s you'd be hard-pressed to find a brook trout, let alone a bug under a stream bed rock. It was a story repeated over and over across the Adirondacks, thanks to industry and its pollution. We just wanted to know where the trout that were being caught in the stream had come from.

I wasn't planning on fishing, I was there to work as far as I was concerned. Holly and our two boys, Jake and Carter, were there, too, so I didn't want to go out into the wilderness to fish and leave them behind at the lodge. On the first day, I stayed around the lodge property while everyone else went out and fished and collected DNA. The problem I found was that until people started coming back from the day with their marked maps and DNA samples, there wasn't anything for me to actually do. And even when they did come back, JP being the data geek that he is had all the collecting and logging well in hand to the point where another hand wasn't needed.

Me being me, I just wanted to get out and help collect the data, also known as fly fishing. And although I was trying not to show my frustrations of sitting idly by looking out at the lake and the stream flowing from it, it must have been fairly obvious.

On the morning of the second day, we were sitting at one of the long tables in the dining hall eating breakfast, and JP introduced me to John Segesta. John was a professional photographer from California, and he was there to shoot photos of what we were doing and possibly write a magazine article about it for The Drake.

John wasn't normally a writer; he spent his time behind a camera for the most part. Pretty seriously, at that. I found out later that he had over two-hundred magazine covers to his credit, not to mention thousands of published photos. Those awe-inspiring shots of athletes doing what they do best in magazine ads and articles in the big publications? Yeah, he's that guy. Top of the game. The problem was, he hadn't gone out with anyone the first day to shoot; he'd stayed at the lodge to capture the venue first.

As we got acquainted over eggs and bacon, JP and my wife both began to pressure me into going out fishing which, obviously, is like trying to get a mouse to eat a piece of cheese. It doesn't matter *what kind of cheese it is*, it's going to gnaw it down to nothing as fast as it can and then expect *more*.

Honestly, at first I dismissed them, telling them I was going to stay around the lodge again to take care of whatever business needed taking care of. But inside I was anxiously waiting for the reason that I *had to go*. And then JP said he had it handled, which he did, and he further stated that John needed to go out and get shots of the stream and some fishing and DNA collection. So, I'd *actually* be doing what needed to be done. I looked at Holly one last time and she smiled and told me she and the boys would be fine. They were going to take a drive, anyway.

I looked at John and asked him when he wanted to leave. He wasn't sold on going out; he said he needed some time to put some stuff together, and he was still on west coast time, jet lag. He *did look* pretty tired. I told him I'd wait and go whenever he was ready. He countered with not wanting to hold me up and that if I was still around when he was done then he'd go, and I countered back with, *"Ok then, I'll be ready when you are."* He finally laughed and said, *"Ok. Gimme a half hour and I'll meet you out side of my cabin."* I went back to ours and strung up my 3wt and unpacked my waders and gear.

We had to drive down a dirt road about a mile, and then park and hike for another mile and a half. Between the drive and the hike, we got to know each other well enough to realize that we were going to get along just fine. It turned out John was there because he'd found JP on social media, and hadn't fished since he was a lot younger, years and years ago. For whatever reason, the images he saw on JP's site struck a chord with him and they ended up talking.

John was looking for something that he'd lost years ago to the professional life. One thing led to another and then he was on a plane; not to shoot some professional athlete for a power bar company, but to photograph some fly anglers in the Adirondacks and feel the warmth of a cork handle in his hand before he went home. When he loaded his gear into my Jeep, it consisted of a large camera bag and a rod tube that JP had given him.

Hiking down the trail, our conversation served to get to know each other a little better - the way all conversations do between two people who find that they get along just fine, even though they've just met. The twenty minutes the hike took flew by because of the stories we shared. Normally, the hike took forever because I just wanted to get to the stream at the end, always thinking the end of the trail was around the next corner. The walking version of *a watched pot never boils,* I guess. By the time we got down to the Cascades, the small waterfall at the bottom of the stream, we knew just enough about each other that we probably could have fooled someone into thinking we'd known each other for a couple years.

The cascades are a small set of natural impoundments at the bottom of the stream, a definitive landmark; more like a red line between two countries on a map, really. Above them is fast moving pocket water. A gravel and sand bottom mixed with rocks and boulders. It flows through dense forest, flanked by second growth pines and a forest floor littered with the rotting carcasses of fallen trees and branches hidden under a world of thick ferns. It's green, dark, and shaded. The quintessential Adirondack brook trout stream.

Below the cascades, the water flows through flat and open country. It winds its way through thick alder choked banks, flat land home to beavers and probably the occasional moose. I've never fished it, for two reasons.

One, the alders are so thick that it's impossible to walk it, let alone navigate through it with a fly rod. Even if you could get to the edge of it on foot it would only take one bad back cast and you'd be cursing for having put in so much work to only break off flies. And two, the only way to fish it would be to float it, and a lot of people float it and fish it from canoes and kayaks. I'm that guy that doesn't like to fish places that everyone else fishes. I may be guilty of actually *not fishing* a spot now and then that I could easily catch a fish from for no other reason than everyone else *does*. I guess sometimes I've been known to not fish particular places like that out of principle alone. I may not be a purist when it comes to fly fishing, but *I do* have my own set of standards. My standards may not always make good sense, but they're mine all the same.

The cascades themselves aren't very big. They're not really big enough to call it a waterfall, but they're not small enough to ignore, either. Basically, from upstream to downstream, they're a rock shelf that funnels the stream down from about twenty-five feet wide to maybe twelve or so, which drops a couple feet into a pool about the size of a big car, like maybe a '68 Chevelle, which then funnels the stream down to about five-feet wide where it pours out over some clogged-up boulders.

It drops about three feet into a mess of white water that only lasts for several feet before calming down as it begins to flow into the open country. It's really a beautiful place and I've probably taken a hundred pictures of it, but they never seem to quite capture the feelings you get when you're standing there. So I always take more each time I go, hoping one will finally do it justice. They never do.

I'd fish them a certain way every time, and so when we got there it was business as usual. I just started to fish. John set his pack down off to the side and started to get his camera gear ready.

I'd always start by stepping out on a large boulder about the size of a kitchen table and tossing a streamer upstream into the white water pummeling itself at the base of the cascades. I'd let the streamer get beat up in the white stuff, pushed down under the worst of it, then strip it out like a minnow retreating downstream in a panic, and finally just let it swing at the end in the calm water passing over a boulder strewn bottom that only shows up in the brightest and highest sun. I'd do that a couple times, then start casting to the left of the white water. Each cast after that, I'd keep casting more to the left until I'd be casting straight out from me. There I'd just let it swing.

I'd usually end up with two or three little brookies standing on that one rock from three different places, or maybe a smallmouth at least. I think there'd only been once or twice that I'd started there and not caught any fish at all. It was pretty dependable. Then I'd move upstream into the middle pool and keep going up from there.

So while John was busy getting his camera out and ready, I stepped onto that big rock. I looked upstream to the white water not more than a dozen feet away or so and peeled a little line of the reel. Then I flipped the streamer out to the white water with about the same enthusiasm that I might show while nonchalantly brushing a fly away from my face. I wasn't really casting, I was simply getting the leader and streamer out away from me to peel more line off the reel to then make a better cast. A *real* cast.

I didn't *need* to make a real cast, I'd already put the streamer in the right place just by flipping it out there. But like I said, even though I'm not a purist, I still have standards. And I really wanted at least a decent back cast before I could admit to actually fishing.

As I lifted the rod to pull the leader from the water for the first *actual cast*, the line went tight. True story. We've all caught a fish when we didn't expect to, I'm sure. You know, like when you're done fishing. You've finally made your last *"one last cast"* and you throw the line back out to reel it in? Only to have a fish come up and smack the fly as it's dragging across the surface like a water skier who has lost their skies but refuses to let go of the rope? Yeah. Well, that's sort of what happened that day. I lifted the line to make the first cast and a fish was tight on the other end already. I laughed out loud, calmly looked over my left shoulder to John and said, *"Well, there's the first fish"* and added some pressure to the leader by lifting.

John spun around, his camera at chest level, viewing screen pointed up at his face as he was changing some settings and had an *"oh crap"* look on his face. He wasn't ready. Of course, neither was I. But here we were.

It was pulling pretty hard and it didn't want to come up. I was only fishing a short 6'6" 3wt with 6X tippet, so I didn't want to pull too hard and break it off, but I was pretty sure it wasn't the fish I was looking for. Which seemed odd to me as I thought it. *"Not the fish I'm after?"* But I was after brook trout and by the weight and fight of the fish, I assumed it was a smallmouth. I looked over my shoulder and told John to not worry about a picture, it was probably just a bass.

But the fish wouldn't come up. It felt like I'd had it on the line for five minutes, but I'd probably only been fighting it for thirty-five seconds in reality when I got a glimpse of it. Time seems to slow down in moments like these. I was still being careful not to lift the rod too hard, figuring it was a smallmouth and considering I had such a light tippet meant for tiny brookies rigged on my most prized fly rod. It was a rod that JP had built for me a few years earlier at the beginning of my fly-fishing affliction, and I didn't want to break it. But when I saw what was on, that all changed.

I did a double take and I think I even unconsciously held my breath when I looked down past my wader boots, past the boulder I was on, and into the fast-moving dark water at the edge of the white stuff. A couple feet down, about where you can just start to make out shapes and some color differences, I saw a fish shape for a quick second. Before my mind could finish remarking *"finally"* to itself, it caught details that set into motion a panic.

The fish was long, but not like a bass. It was more of a torpedo shape looking straight down on it, but it twisted its body like a shark turns as it circles for another bite. Bass are too flat, I think, to turn like that; at least I don't ever remember seeing one do it. *But trout do.* I also noticed two dark red fins out to its sides, only slightly lighter in color from the rest of its dark body from this angle. And they were trimmed in arctic white. It was a brook trout. I believe the first words to come out of my mouth upon recognizing it were *"holy shit,* or *"oh shit."* Something along those lines.

I repeated it several times and turned back to John, who now had a look of concern on his face. He was still setting up his camera. *"This is a serious fish, you've got to get a shot of it somehow before I lose it!"* But as he came running to my side, the panic got the better of me as I heard my own voice echo the two most frightening words in what I'd said, *"Lose it."*

To lose this trout would've been the single biggest tragedy to ever befall me on any piece of water, anywhere to this point. Plus, there were a whole bunch of anglers to meet back up with later that evening who'd never believe it if there wasn't a photo of it in my hands. And so, I did what I did out of the shear fear of losing the trout and fear alone…I pulled up hard on the 3wt, ripped my net from its waiting place tucked in my wading belt on my back side and scooped up the brookie in one swift motion. It barley fit in my little net.

I was used to catching the typical little brookies from this stream. You know, they normally range anywhere from three or four inches up to ten or eleven. And an eleven-inch brook trout from a little stream like this is a *trophy* fish. It didn't get much better than an eleven-inch wild brook trout. At least that's what I'd *thought* up to this moment.

I couldn't believe I'd caught a brookie that I could actually hold by the tail with my other hand under its head, and even more unbelievable was how I had caught it. In my mind, I wasn't even fishing yet, I was *getting ready* to fish. Some days it's better to be lucky than good. I stand by that statement and I use it enough on the water that I guess you could say it's kind of my motto. If the shoe fits...

There were a few pictures taken, but I think that goes without saying under the circumstances. I also made sure to both mentally take a picture in my mind of where the fish's tail ended on my arm with its head even with the end of my fingertips, and to also have my fly rod parallel to my lucky catch as well in a photo. I'd measure off the fly rod using the picture later when I could find a measuring tape. I can still see the fish alongside my arm today as if it happened yesterday, its bottom jaw even with the tip of my index finger and the end of its tail more than an inch past my elbow.

In all honesty, it was most definitely the luckiest catch I've ever had, simply because the fish would've had no problem snapping that 6X tippet like Hulk Hogan could snap Pee-Wee Herman's arm if he'd ever tried to reach out and stroke his championship belt. Between the size of the brook trout and its sharp teeth that should have easily popped the gossamer leader, and the delicate 3wt graphite rod that had been doubled over - bent right in half for a few seconds - I should've never landed that fish. I credit it to luck. But analyzing it further, I did come up with a better excuse, at least equal to being lucky if nothing more. And probably just as impressive in an uninspiring way.

It all happened so fast that neither the fish nor I knew what was going on. That was it. Had I realized, thought it out and let the fish pull line and tire itself, it would've raked its teeth across the leader and been free with a single head shake. Or simply poured on the juice and gone beyond the limits of the tiny strand of nylon with a little effort. And had the fish had enough time to realize that it was stuck to the end of something from the world above, it would've had more than enough time - mere seconds - to enact either of the scenarios and been gone. It just happened too fast for either of us to think. The fish didn't know what was going on until it was too late, and I didn't either.

After reviving and releasing the fish, I made some casts to the pool just above the boulders and managed another brookie, nowhere near the size of the first, of course. Which was really something to think about because on any other day, the second fish would have been a dandy. A really pretty nine-incher. Beautiful spots, chaotic mottling covering its back like the camo netting the military uses to hide vehicles and camps from aircraft, and fins trimmed in bright crisp white. It was really a nice fish. But my hands were still shaking and my heart still pounding from that first one.

The rest of the trip upstream I fished, and John hung back with his camera and did his thing. This was also the trip upstream that I started to feel like I'd spent too much time on this stretch, because it seemed too easy. I knew the stream pretty damn well by now, which I guess is why JP wanted John to go out with me; but I'd never really thought about how well I knew it until I started to call the fish like a pool shark calls *eight ball, corner pocket.*

I'd tell him something like, *"I'm going to go crouch in the ferns on the bank near that rotting pine and get a brookie from the pocket behind that boulder,"* and then go do exactly that. I was afraid he was getting the wrong impression of me. After all, I had started out with that monster, and then moved upstream like a vacuum salesman knocking on doors knowing which house would have someone home every time. I tried to explain to him that I really just fished the stream a lot. Put me somewhere else and I'd just be another idiot getting beat by fish with brains the size of M&Ms.

Probably my favorite moment on the stream that day, besides the first brookie, was when John put down his camera and rigged up the 3wt that JP had given him. He told me that he hadn't fished in years, and by "years" he didn't mean four or five, he meant *years*. So, when he finally took a break from shooting photos and started casting, I moved upstream from him a little ways but kept watching.

His first few casts were rough, but still more than adequate to get the fly out there where the fish were on such a small stream...which is part of the beauty of fishing small streams. You're not looking for distance in your cast as much as accuracy. And accuracy comes easier when the target isn't so far away. The fishing was so good that day that it didn't take long at all - a matter of minutes - before John had a small brookie dancing at the end of his leader. I know that stream like the back of my hand, but it's not just where the fish are. Sometimes, specific events engrain themselves in your mind. Precise, detailed memories from great days.

Along our path that day, a family of mergansers, a mother and three ducklings swimming single file behind her, were in a shallow pool. A pool I wanted to cast to just below a huge boulder. It's more than just a huge boulder, it's a landmark on the stream. The boulder is the size of a school bus, and on its upstream side is a log jam piled against it that's almost every bit as dense as the boulder itself. I imagine the logs have been piling up against it during the spring thaws and summer storms for a hundred years or more easily. Probably longer. Like, since forever.

Anyway, as the mother duck spotted us coming in her direction, she hurried her ducklings upstream around the boulder where they were out of sight. I told John I wanted to hang back and let the pool rest, that the merganser had probably done a good job of spooking all the fish in it. We waited a few minutes and then as we started to move in, I saw movement in the trees above the stream on the other side of the boulder where the ducks had disappeared.

A Bald Eagle dropped from a high branch and glided upstream and out of sight. It was really something. The bird was big, but it looked even bigger with its wings stretched outright as if trying to touch the tree branches reaching over the stream from either side. The canopy formed a thick green tunnel over the stream and the eagle seemed to take up all the empty space. Knowing the merganser and her ducklings were on the other side of the boulder, I softly said to her under my breath, *"You're welcome. If it wasn't for us, you and your babies would be an eagle's dinner today."*

So there was the big fish at the Cascades, then the eagle, and then finally there was John standing on a rock with water moving by him and a brookie on the end of his line. I like to think that John has specific memories from that day as well, and that his favorite started when he put down his camera.

Later that evening, he brought out his camera and everyone got a glimpse of that brookie. JP just shook his head and grinned, but I just played it off as a lucky day; which was really all any good day of fishing is, I don't care how smart you think you are. I've seen really unlucky days, which means there's always the exact opposite as well. Really lucky.

A week or so later, John sent me a few shots in an email, so I went to the garage and got a tape measure and got out that 3wt. When I measured the fly rod where the fish started and stopped in the photos, it was somewhere around twenty-two inches. Then I remembered where it came to on my arm, just past my elbow, and measured that, too. That measurement came in at almost twenty inches, but not quite. So I split the difference and claimed it to be a twenty-one-inch small stream brookie. But more often than not, I remember it being much longer, like around twenty-three or twenty-four inches. Fish rarely get smaller over time.

Twenty, twenty-one, maybe twenty-two inches of luck. With a little panic thrown in for good measure. I've made a hundred casts to the white water at the bottom of the Cascades since that day, but I've never seen another brook trout over ten inches in that spot. Or *anywhere* on the stream for that matter. Yes indeed, some days it's better to be lucky than good.

11

No Hope

*In the spring of 2017, my wife told me late one evening that she wanted to separate. We'd been together for seventeen years. I was devastated. For the next year, I struggled to find my place, and even fly fishing seemed hopeless to me where in the past it had always offered hope when nothing else did. When I was able to pull words out of my head, they were honest, but not light-hearted tales of hope and joy as they had been. There was a lot of symbolism, dark and depressing. But I still wrote, all be it only a fraction of how frequently I had in the past. Most days it just wasn't there. Nothing was. *

I texted JP saying I was taking off for a couple days. Someone should know where I was going to be. My wife didn't care, but someone should know. I drove north, a familiar place with brook trout and no cell coverage. I pitched a one-man pup tent, arranged a ring of river stones, and gathered a little fire wood. A bottle of whiskey stood on the ground next to the back tire of the Jeep.

I sat in silence and stared at the bottle, not really looking at it at all. Eventually, I strung up a fly rod. It was the first time I'd come up to this river and not actually cared about fishing. I was there, just going through the motions I suppose. Because I didn't know what else to do.

How many times had I been up this stream? A couple, at least. Enough to say I knew it, I'd fished it before, and I knew what was around the next bend. The water might be a little higher or a little lower than the time before, but I'd seen it. Maybe too many times.

As I released another fish back into a familiar pool, I found that I wasn't questioning whether it was a wild fish or not, but instead if I really wanted to fish this same stretch anymore. Some streams you can fish your entire life and never get tired of them, and others...well, once you've seen them - once you've learned their curves and bends, found their deep pools and slow runs - maybe they just don't interest you anymore. Maybe you begin to think it's time to move on. I broke my fly off on the same damn tree I had the last time I was here and thought to myself, *shouldn't you have seen that coming*? Same old story.

I made a last-minute decision to walk up to Reeds Pond in the final remaining daylight. I wasn't sure why, but then again I wasn't sure of a lot of stuff lately. My feet carried me in that direction, so I just followed. There were so many bugs in the air that they seemed to outnumber the stars in the perfectly clear Adirondack sky, and when the pond came into view I saw it boiling like a pot of water on a stove. I'd caught a brookie out of the pond once, but only once. So naturally I wondered what was rising. Certainly, they couldn't all be brookies. I'd only ever caught one here out of a hundred casts.

I made a few casts with a dry fly that might have been just a little too big, or maybe just not the right pattern. Or it could've just been that I'd never been a good dry fly angler, and now I felt even less confidant on a still water. Where to cast? Anywhere? There was no current and the fish rose randomly everywhere. I finally caught a break when several fish rose in one place and I made a decent cast and found a small chub at hand in the end. Not that I had anything against chubs, but I just looked at it as another sign. Perhaps it's time to move on.

Back at the campsite, I started a little fire at the back of the Jeep, but I wasn't sure why. A granola bar for dinner didn't require a fire, and while I did have a folding camp stool, the black flies were so bad that I didn't see myself sitting out for more than a few minutes before going insane. I guess I was lighting a fire because that's just what you do when you're camping. It's an expected routine thing. You've always done it, so whether you need one or not, it just seems the thing to do. It passes time anyhow. You have to do something.

I waited until the sun was almost gone - just dark enough for the black flies to disappear for the night - before I opened the Jeep's back hatch and laid out my sleeping bag inside. On the hood rested my strung up 3wt and 5wt. I figured out there in the middle of nowhere they'd be safe from thieves, no need to lock them up. Inside I could hear the river just outside rushing over rocks and on downstream just like the other times I'd camped here. Same old story.

The river flows by like you're not even there, like you don't even matter. Sometimes you need these realizations to put your life into perspective. Next to the river, you're small and insignificant. It'll be there long after you're gone. With any luck, so will the brookies - which anglers will still chase - while your name is inevitably forgotten. I slept next to the river in the back of the Jeep, my pillow a rolled-up sweatshirt next to a tool box, next to a pile of rod tubes and my damp waders.

In the morning, I woke up with a stiff neck and a sore hip to the sound of birds all around. The sun was just beginning to illuminate the sky, and then the birds quieted down. It was as if they all woke each other up, which I suppose isn't so farfetched. After a granola bar breakfast, I had a bend in the 3wt and a brookie on the line, out of the same pocket behind the same boulder I always found one in. Same old stream, same old story. I loaded up the Jeep and looked at the atlas in the pile of stuff in the passenger seat. Perhaps it was time to find someplace new, which, in itself, was again the same old story.

A few days later, I found myself walking a trail close to home. Not because I wanted to go fishing, but because I didn't want to be home. And there was no one there to miss me anyhow.

I carried my 6wt at my side with a casualness that said I was going fishing, but I didn't really care. I just put one foot in front of the other, the same way I would anywhere else where I had no place to be and no reason to get anywhere.

The ticks had been horrible. Everyone you talked to had either pulled them off themselves or their kids that year so far. And while I'd never had one on me in 41 years, both Jacob and Carter had found them on their clothes one night as they got ready for their showers. They'd yelled from the bathroom that there was a spider on the floor, but sure enough, they learned what a tick looked like, luckily without needing one removed. The ticks had been horrible, yet I walked on through knee-deep grass in shorts and sandals, not much caring what attached itself to me.

I walked a dark trail, closed in by trees drooping and reaching, green and cool blocking the sunlight. They wanted it all for themselves. At my feet was a narrow path of dirt - a single track of game trail, more or less - that the odd human beings would use to their advantage. It fought to stay clear, flanked by knee high grass threatening to fill it in.

The path was interrupted here and there by the deep puddles that were left behind by the ruts of farm tractors in years past. As I approached them, the frogs would jump from their resting places at the puddle's edges and bury themselves in the muck on the bottom. I watched one leap a good three feet and then come to rest perfectly in a deer track pressed into the mud only a couple inches below the surface of the stagnant water. I saw the similarities in the frogs diving for cover, trying to become invisible in a world where everything seemed out to get them, and the idea that I was merely trying to disappear - at least for a short time - from a life that seemed hell bent on making me cry uncle.

Ahead of me, a rabbit made a single jump from the middle of the trail into the undergrowth on the left. It looked like the dolphins I'd watched in the Gulf of Mexico years ago as they leapt from the waves. Its body appeared momentarily as it sailed out of the tall grass, arched as it made its descent back into the green and was gone. It never made a sound. Just gone.

I had a fly box full of streamers, a box of nymphs, and a box of dries, but I knew the streamer caught in the hook keeper above the cork handle would probably be the only thing I'd fish. I had grabbed the small pack with all the fly boxes out of routine, nothing more. There wasn't much concern for variety in the decision. I just didn't seem to care about much of anything. I was going through motions. I walked, knowing where I'd end up, but without a plan and little concern for anything involved. It was hot. At least I could stand in the water.

At the end of the wooded path, I came to the old dam and it looked about how it always looked. A long gray concrete ramp, still water above, water trickling over the length of it and ending in a small swirling of water softly frothing at the bottom. In some places, saturated moss clung thinly to the manmade structure. It waited there quietly as if to not draw any attention, but ready for one wrong step or one moment of distraction to send me sliding into the shallow water below.

Logs, tree trunks, and all sorts of drift wood rested high centered on the dam's top, along with the ever-present man-made garbage that you inevitably find wherever water flows. I couldn't help but realize how the masses of hung-up dead wood resembled my life. Just a bunch of old crap, teetering on the edge, waiting for the water to raise once more and send it all sliding and tumbling down. Downstream into the unknown. There I was, looking out at it and comparing it to my life. Me, the freaking poet. I hated myself for it.

I thought I'd cut through the woods and get just downstream of the dam and around the first bend. It was a favorite spot where the wide water below the dam narrowed to no more than twenty feet from an easy seventy feet, a spot where there were always smallmouth tucked against the far cutout bank in the twisted and tangled tree roots, just above the ball of driftwood that was always there. For all the water level changes through all the seasons, that pile of driftwood always seemed consistently there. It always seemed the same. It never got bigger, never got smaller, it was just always there. And so were a few bass. It was dependable if nothing else.

As I broke through the undergrowth to the sandy beach, my eyes fell on sticks standing upright in the sand. Three huge spinning rods were supported in the crotches of the sticks, and three fishermen stood off to the side talking. Budweiser cans, cigarette butts, and two blue plastic worm containers tossed to the side telling me they wouldn't be leaving when the fishermen did. A stringer absolutely full of fish, all bass and carp, was staked in the sand at the river's edge.

While I don't hold it against another angler who takes a fish home for dinner, I also couldn't help but think that my dependable spot was ruined for the day by human beings who'd probably tell you how much they loved the spot while at the same time leaving their trash behind and keeping every fish they caught regardless of legal limits or ethics. I silently stepped back into the undergrowth after staring for a moment. They never saw me. I wished I'd never seen them.

Back on top the dam, my shins and calves scraped up and stinging from pushing through the heavy ground cover by the river, I stood and surveyed the water. I was looking for signs of fish, but really not caring if I saw anything or not. The weed beds were coming up pretty strong now. It'd be best to fish something weed less for bass or pike here, or maybe dries for pan fish or carp feeding on the top, but I just stood there. The water flowed through my sandals, around my feet, and down the dam behind me.

In front of me, a carp cruised by, and then two more. I thought about casting out in front of them, giving them a dead bait fish imitation lying on the bottom to come across. There was no time for anything else. I knew how far in front of them I needed to cast, about where they'd be and when. I didn't cast. I couldn't explain it and didn't even try to. I just didn't cast. My arm felt heavy with a fly rod weighing only ounces. There was no motivation to make a cast. I figured the little gray and white streamer was a long shot at best anyhow. In reality, there was no hope at the end of this cast. So, I simply stood there and watched them go by.

I'd been here before, stood in this very place, and watched this very same thing happen. Cruising carp. Nothing at the end of the cast. Maybe in the beginning there was hope, but after long enough - after enough casts - the hope would be gone, and I'd just be casting out of desperation at best. I'd run out of even desperation now, without a single cast.

I stood there and thought about other places I'd fished and had better luck and wondered why I wasn't standing at one of those places instead. I couldn't come up with an answer; this was just one of those places I always ended up. After I moved down to the far end of the dam, I did finally make a cast and there was a small bass at the end of my line. But it didn't do anything for me. Like I said, I'd been here before. I knew what to expect.

I thought about going someplace else, but it was too late. The walk back would take too long, and the day would be over before I could get somewhere else. A plane flew overhead. A U-Haul truck passed over the bridge on the other side of the river. I thought about places I could go. Places I'd never been. Places I could escape to, or places I could disappear in like a rabbit in the brush or a frog in a hoof print in the bottom of a stagnant puddle. There was a large pond fairly close by where I had never fished, but always wondered about. Even if I could be on the other side of the country tomorrow, would it even make a difference?

There were rivers in Montana or even Colorado that I'd never seen. There was a lake in Nevada where anglers waded out into the water with step ladders and used them as casting perches for monster trout. There were steelhead in the Pacific Northwest, I've read about them hundreds of times. There were peacock bass in southern Florida now. Patagonia could even be within walking distance if one put their mind to it, I supposed. After all, you've got the rest of your life to get there. And here I stood on an old shitty *dam*. How many times had I been here, and how many times did I have to stand here before I realized I could be somewhere else? The carp cruised by again. Three big fish cruising along, indifferent to the angler, with seemingly nowhere to go and all day to get there.

Fast forward a couple months...

Spur of the moment. It was the only way I hit the water anymore. Before, I'd been able to plan it - at least a day ahead maybe - but not anymore. When life falls apart, there's no planning anything. Everything crumbles around you and you're lucky to just scoop up a crumb here or there when you can. My appetite had wasted away like my optimism. One real meal a day, usually a sandwich at lunch. The rest of my nutrition was absorbed out of the whiskey and potato chips I mostly ate for dinner those days. But the water. Yea, spur of the moment at best. When it wasn't high and brown from the rain.

A Monday after work. It hadn't rained in a few days, about four I figured. That was amazing in itself, seeing how all spring and summer it had rained every other day. It was our first beautiful weekend that I could remember that summer so far. I met JP up in Old Forge on a Saturday for the debut of JP Ross's new venture, Trail Marker. He was breaking into the adventure camper trailer market, a guy that wasn't happy sitting still. I sat next to it at a small outdoors show and talked to people, thinking I was just far enough from home - hoping I was - so that I wouldn't have to talk to anyone I knew.

The Trail Marker was a big hit and it got me thinking. I needed to do something. Anything. Make some money. Go fishing somewhere far away. If I could do both together, that'd be great; but I'd settle for one or the other at this point. I had no direction, and motivation had been at an all-time low. It got me thinking that obviously my life wasn't what I wanted it to be, and I wasn't getting any younger. The aging process seemed to be speeding up, actually.

Then the next morning, I woke up to a view of the fog rolling off of Fourth Lake, and covering the tops of the mountains surrounding it, and a loon hanging out by the dock, and it just all came down on me at once. I didn't cry. I hadn't yet, which I thought was odd. But I had to do something. And fishing seemed like a good something to start with. It'd been weeks. Like I said, motivation had been at an all-time low. I couldn't believe I was trying to *convince* myself to *go fishing*.

I hadn't moved out of the house yet; I was still holding on to hope, so I just took up residence on a futon in the basement. The boys knew something was up but weren't saying anything. And I was waiting for her to finally tell me to just get out in no uncertain terms. Kicked out of my own home. I kept the whiskey bottles hidden under the futon, but they were always there.

When I walked in the house after work and no one was home, that spur of the moment thing happened. I didn't even think about going fishing during the day. I didn't think about it on the drive home, even though streamers waved and danced, stuck on the dash, as if trying to get my attention. I mostly just stared out the windshield lately, pondering my place in the world, not paying much attention to the feathers and fur and all the colors. They just got in the way when I tried to eject a tape from the cassette player. Usually because the song made me think of stuff I didn't want to think about.

Have you ever heard a song a thousand times over your life - like, say, Black Sabbath's *"Paranoid"* - only to suddenly hear it one day like it's the first time? Suddenly, the words hit you differently; it's not just rock and roll anymore. You want to eject the tape, but as the hackles and buck tail from the bass streamers cover up the eject button, you pull your hand back. You'll finish the song, after all. It's like the universe wanted you to hear it to the end.

There was no one home, and then suddenly, I saw the creek in my mind as I stared into the quiet and empty living room. And just like that, I threw on a pair of shorts, tightened the Velcro straps of my sandals, and got back in the Jeep.

I found myself by the home team dugout at the ball field, stringing up my 7wt two minutes later. "Paranoid" was still playing in my head but beginning to fade out; it was gone when I took my first step into sunlit clear water. The water was slow in this spot, and the rings sent out as I waded in reflected the sunlight on the rocky bottom, as if scanning for life as they traveled out, finally diminishing and then disappearing back into the surface, like they'd been turned off.

I stood in a waist-deep slow current. The sun was bright, warm, and the water perfect. I made a cast to the opposite side of the creek, just next to a dead fall washed up on the bank, and I never even got to make the first strip. The line went tight, and I set the hook.

It was just one of those afternoons where every time you thought a spot looked fishy, it was. If there was a shaded spot along the bank, the line went tight almost as soon as the Woolly Bugger hit the water. If there was a deep run in the middle, out in the sun, and if it was deep enough to hold back some of the light (just be a little darker than the water around it), the line would go tight.

Mostly smallmouths. A couple times it was a good-sized fallfish, which fight almost just as hard. Life in the creek was on the move, and there seemed to be no time to waste. While you stood in the shallows admiring a fish in your hand, you felt crayfish trying to take cover under your toes or heel. Birds zoomed up and down the creek. A deer flicked its ear giving away its position in the brush. Life was on the move. No time to waste.

And then, below the bridge in town as I stripped in a crayfish pattern made of marabou and chenille with dumbbell eyes for weight, I saw it. I was waist deep. I'd just let a ten-inch smallie go not ten seconds earlier when something long and dark caught my eye resting on the bottom. It wasn't far away, fifteen feet maybe. It was facing me - there was no way it hadn't seen me - but it was one of those fish that doesn't spook easily, and even if you did spook it, it wasn't going to show it. I froze.

I knew I only had one larger streamer in my fly box, so I moved my hands slowly up to my chest pack and began the task of snipping off the crayfish pattern and tying on the five-inch streamer tied entirely of flash. No deer hair. No Hackles. No marabou or even fake craft fur from the craft store. Nothing but flash. A black back, a blue mid-section, and a silver belly. I made a short cast just above it and out in the current, and as it sunk, it passed the fish on the bottom at about its eleven o'clock. The fish turned to face it and stared it down like a top predator does. I gave a twitch.

Where the dark colors of the fish blended in to the darkness of the bottom quite well, the stripes of the tiger muskie were illuminated by the sun penetrating the depth. It looked fast, like a drag car with flashy graphics ready to launch off the line. I gave another twitch and it glided forward. I didn't know what to do. Leave it be, twitch it again, or strip fast? I had to make a decision. Now.

I chose strip fast, thinking that predators chased prey, and prey taking flight usually triggered something in the predator. You don't run from a dog, it'll run you down. You don't run from a grizzly, it'll run you down. Even a damn house cat - when it's in the right mood, acting on its primal instincts - if you run, it'll chase you down. I stripped fast. The fish glided forward into darkness not ten feet away from me and was gone.

I wasn't surprised, not at all. And I honestly wasn't disappointed. I almost knew it was going to happen from the very moment I'd spotted the fish, but I'd taken the time to change flies anyway, and I'd made the cast anyway. I wasn't afraid of failure because it didn't matter, and I'd forgotten about everything that did. And that's exactly what I needed to do. I needed to find something to motivate me to make a decision and act on it, instead of just sitting on my ass and fearing the future. I needed a reason to make a cast, whether it ended well or not. I had to make the cast. I needed the hope the cast offered.

On my way back upstream, I caught a few more bass. One of them had a good scar between its dorsal fin and its head, one that started at the top and continued down more than halfway to its underside. I'd seen it a couple times on the creek that year. They were talon scars from the Osprey that lived on the cell tower on the other side of the highway and hunted this stretch of the creek. It was a pretty gnarly scar and I figured he probably used it to pick up the lady bass, because chicks dig scars.

It also occurred to me that the scars were proof that sometimes when you think it's the end, when you suddenly feel yourself being ripped out of the world you know, maybe it isn't the end just yet after all. Maybe you live to fight the current another day. To make more casts. Me, the freaking poet again.

******

I opened my eyes to almost complete darkness, coming out of one of those sleeps that was heavy enough to make you forget where you were for a few seconds. It was near pitch dark and I could barely make out the silhouette of the Yeti cup on the coffee table next to me, an arm's reach away. I was on a couch, twisted up in an old army surplus sleeping bag. *OK, I was in a basement on a couch.* Now I remembered. I slept well. Must have been just enough whiskey the night before. Or too much. I guessed it depended on how you looked at it.

I rolled over and closed my eyes again, not really thinking I should go back to sleep because I wasn't awake enough to actually rationalize, but then the thoughts entered my semi-conscious brain. It was before sunrise...*you're awake early enough, you should probably go fishing.* I reached over and blindly felt for my phone in the dark. What time was it? When the screen lit up in front of my face, it was blinding. My eyes struggled to bring anything into focus, but there was a message. *Check out this video of Greenland.*

There's something about the combination of living in someone's basement on a couch, and a spectacular video shared by someone on the other side of the world of fishing in yet some other country, that can really do things inside your head. *To the inside of your head.* I felt like a waste laying there on the couch in the dark with the tiny screen in front of me. The footage of mountains flanking a river valley in Greenland, eagles soaring, chasing arctic char. It put me in my place. Which is to say, it told me at 5:35am on a Saturday morning, I was *not* in my place.

I got up. It was still dark. Good. I went out to the Jeep and as the engine fired up, and the power made it to the radio, Gloria Gaynor was belting out *"I Will Survive."* My hand went for the tuning buttons but then pulled back. It was cheesy. A little painful. Ironic. But it fit on so many levels. I let it play to the end on my way out of the neighborhood. Then the DJ rolled into REO Speedwagon's *"Keep on Loving You"* and I decided there were too many songs about love and not enough about fishing. I pushed the tape into the tape deck and AC/DC wailed *"If You Want Blood, You Got It."*

We've got a few well-known local creeks here, and for no apparent reason I drove to one that I hadn't fished since I was in high school. Let's just say that was a long time ago. A *long* time ago. I parked behind a bar and for the next hour, as the sun crept up, I made halfhearted casts to pools and riffles that looked fishy enough but didn't seem to hold any fish. I'm not saying there weren't any. I know they're in that creek. I just couldn't find them. I wasn't really into it, I guess. I was just going through the motions.

The trash twisted in all the trees from the flooding that had raised the creek over ten feet during the summer, the cell tower and the changing LED billboard visible past the bridge looking south, the taillights and bumpers of the cars looking down on me from the car dealership lots that butted up to the creek, the noise of the traffic passing by. They just weren't what I was looking for, I suppose. I was still on a creek with a fly rod, but when it's not doing anything for me – which, for the record, had never happened before this mess - it's seriously time to do...*something*.

Back in the Jeep, back to the neighborhood. I was going back to the couch when I decided I wasn't done and pulled off the road next to one of our other, probably better-known, creeks. I tied on a crayfish pattern with dumbbell eyes and fished the drop off on the edge of a sand bar. I stripped the fly across the bottom at a snail's pace in a place that was too dark and deep to see the bottom. If I couldn't see anything, then I could only imagine there must be fish there. I needed that more than to be able to see that there really wasn't anything down there at this point. When the line went tight I breathed a sigh of relief.

Three fish. I got to see three fish. The first two were decent smallmouths. *Decent* meaning they were smallmouths; they were real, and they were on my line. The third fish was a nice fall fish around fifteen inches, give or take. I got them each within a few feet of me. I lost all three right there when the tippet broke, or my bad knots let go. Whichever it was, after the third one I decided to let the whole thing go. I walked back to the Jeep and spent the rest of the day watching my oldest son's soccer and then double-header baseball games.

I stood there trying to be invisible to the other parents, watching kids having fun on the winning side and kicking dirt on the losing side. I'd been on both sides too many times to count or even remember in life. I'm not sure if I was kicking dirt after losing all three of those fish, or if I was just indifferent to the whole experience. But I was still thinking about those arctic char in Greenland. And was wondering where I put that little book of fishing knots that I bought a few months earlier.

12

Dry Flies

I went to look at an apartment that was a thirty-minute drive from work. I understand that to some people, a thirty-minute commute is nothing; that some people are used to six lane traffic and a couple hours a day spent glaring through the windshield just trying to get somewhere they'd rather not go to. Then they try to escape the same place at the end of the day. But I live in Upstate N.Y. I'd had several jobs over my somewhat comical and at other times depressing - but never normal - life; for the most part, through those several jobs, I'd never had to drive more than twenty minutes to get to work. For one of them, if I put the gas pedal to the floor I could make it in just under four minutes.

The apartment was on the West Canada Creek, so in all honesty, I'd probably have considered closer to an hour's drive if it had worked out. But the guy who was supposed to show it to me never showed up, so I took it as a sign. Anyone who was going to expect me to pay the rent on time but couldn't keep his own schedule was someone I'd probably butt heads with eventually.

I sat in the driveway for half an hour, waiting. I stared out the Jeep's windshield at the wide river ironically named a creek, considering how great it would be to come home, step into waders and then into the water not sixty feet from the back door and get skunked by stocked trout on a daily basis. When I gave up hope and left, I decided I couldn't make the drive and not cast a line, so I pulled into the fishing access lot I hadn't fished from in three years.

I watched a fisherman drown worms for another half hour before he himself gave up and left. The whole time he was hoping a trout would find his worm held on the bottom by a row of slip shot crimped twelve inches above it, I was watching the occasional fish rise out farther in the slow and smooth current. When I wasn't looking for a rise, I was watching the tiny tan caddis flies - probably a size nineteen or twenty - fluttering about, seeming to be in a hurry flying at angles not quite parallel to the water, but not steep enough to get them very high into the air either. Just when you think you're struggling in life, it might do you some good to go sit by a river and watch a caddis fly struggle to get off the water and go nowhere in particular at a painfully slow and erratic pace. It kind of puts things into perspective.

It also helps to make you feel a little better - and dare I take the chance in saying a little smarter, even though I know I'm a moron in most matters - to sit and watch someone failing with live bait when the answer is happening right in front of them. You see the rises. You see the bugs. You have a 5wt in the Rod Vault on the roof and a couple tiny caddis dries stuck in the foam on the dash. You see the universe at work in front of you while the fisherman in the lawn chair can't see why a trout won't eat that worm. You want to raise your hand like the kid in grade school you hated that always had all the answers and looked so smug when your answer was wrong and his was right. *"Oh, oh, oh! I know! I know! I know!"*

Instead, I sat patiently...watching fish rise, watching birds swoop at the same bugs the trout let slip by, watching the frustrated fisherman shake his head in disgust. It's not really that I was patient. I knew that I had the formula and that I'm a horrible dry fly fisherman, regardless. I figured I'd probably get skunked all the same, by stocked fish no less. Even though I knew exactly what was going on.

Finally, the fisherman stood up and stretched his back, dumped out his worms, reeled in his line, and headed for his old Crown Vic with the fading navy-blue paint and vinyl top. I stepped out of the Jeep and he gave me a nod. *"Good luck, I give up."* I couldn't tell if he said it as if he didn't think I could do any better, or because he figured I'd go out there and catch what he couldn't; but I've never seen an elderly guy toss a lawn chair in the back seat and peel out in a cloud of dust from a gravel lot in quite such a perfectly miserable...well, if a car can have body language, it said he was done fishing. Forever.

I pulled on my waders, took my time snipping off and then tying on a slightly longer length of 6X tippet, and then pulled a fly from the dash. I didn't know what had been getting into me lately, but I didn't just keep streamers anymore. I always seemed to have a couple dries stuck on the dash, in the headliner, or on the little piece of foam glued to the brim of my ball cap. That's a couple more than I used to keep around, which was none. I even had floatant in the glovebox. It was still full and so old that the label had been gone for a couple years, but it was always there. I never took it out as if in the back of my mind I figured someday I'd *get into this whole dry fly thing*.

I was in the river for few minutes, I'd made a handful of casts, and I was actually impressed with myself that I was *almost* making good natural drifts. Almost. I was thinking to myself about something that has now escaped my memory, but I know it had me distracted just enough that the splash out where my fly was made me flinch. I laughed out loud as I lifted the rod. I don't know why; sometimes you just have to laugh, and what's better to laugh at than yourself?

The little nine-inch stocked fish jumped a good three times. He didn't know he was small, he just knew he didn't want to go where this bug was pulling him.

I made a couple more casts and then I just turned and walked out of the river. That's about the time I realized the old man hadn't left completely. He was sitting just up the gravel road, watching me in his mirror, and he waved his hand out the window as he pulled away. It might have been a middle finger, but I'd like to think it was just a friendly *"nice job"* kind of wave. I had been on both ends. I'd muttered under my breath when I was the other guy, and I'd offered my spot to the other guy as well. All I really knew was that I was looking for an apartment, preferably on a river, preferably stocked with dumb fish that from time to time would make me feel smarter. It was a decent formula, almost as good as the ones presented to you on a river from time to time that make you think you have the universe figured out.

13

Green Lake

I had been living in my friend Chris's basement now for about three months. Maybe more. Time was being lost, nothing mattered to me, and so there seemed no reason to keep track of it. We'd known each other since the seventh grade and when it came down to me getting kicked out of my own house, Chris and his wife Kelly were adamant that I stay with them for a while as I tried to figure life out. I declined at first, as I looked for an apartment, but wasn't having much luck finding anything I could see myself living in. I eventually caved in and moved into a basement room with a garage entrance and a sleeper couch.

Actually, there were three couches arranged in a U shape around a coffee table, so I had my choice of three different couches to sleep on. Two happened to be pull-out beds, which I refused to pull out on principle alone. If I was going to live in a basement, I was going to sleep on a couch.

On the coffee table in the middle of the room always sat my fly-tying vice and a mess of scattered materials, and a bottle of whiskey in any form other than full and unopened. I was tying and getting out to fish as much as I could because eventually it finally began to take my mind off things again, the way it used to before the whole separation thing. And before the whole separation thing turned into the whole divorce thing. I was looking for an apartment, toying around with the idea of buying a house, and spending a lot of time pouring whiskey and tying flies.

The only downfall to living in their basement - besides the divorce itself - was that they were a happy young family upstairs, and I was downstairs listening to what my own house sounded like years ago with our first child learning to walk and play. I didn't go upstairs much. They'd make dinner and invite me up, and sometimes I'd stay up there and watch a movie with them after their daughter had gone to sleep.

I tried, for the most part, be an invisible guest. It was as much to not be an intruder in *their family lives* as it was to not be reminded of *my own*. So I was going out to fish as much as I could when I wasn't with my own boys. Or at my cousin's bar that was only about twenty minutes north. I'd go fish the West Canada Creek, then stop at the *16 Stone* in Holland Patent on my way home. I honestly didn't drink much there because I knew I was going to have to drive. I mainly sat at the end of the bar and thought about everything I didn't want to think about. Divorce is a hell of a thing.

JP and I got a text one night from our good buddy, John Montefusco, who happened to be at a fundraiser up in the Adirondacks. He wanted to know if we were both free on a specific late summer weekend because he was going to bid on a weekend trip for a private club up there. He ended up outbidding the competition so that we could do a guy's weekend in a cabin on a huge private club with lots of fishing surrounding us. The timing couldn't have been much better. But I guess when it comes down to it, what are friends for if you can't mooch fishing trips off them during one of the worst times in your life?

There's a lot to be said about a cabin with nothing in the middle of nowhere. And it begins with the drive in on an old two-track splashing through mud holes and puddles. The drive may have only been the beginning of the weekend, but it can sometimes be the beginning of the best part.

What I'm referring to is that first moment on the drive when you cross that line, that place when you're suddenly aware that you're cut off from civilization. That you're *out there*. And it feels *awesome*. The cell phone gets shut off and tossed in the glove box. It's no use out here to look for an email or attempt a call. There are no cell towers, only mountains and trees and lakes and rivers. Trout and bears and moose, fly rods and a bottle of bourbon sitting on a table in a dimly lit cabin with a wood stove off in the corner.

There was no pavement to make the ride smooth. No white lines to stay between and no yellow lines to keep you on your side. It was up to you to pay attention, to pick your safe speed. To avoid the rocks pushing up from below and the deep mud holes that threatened to hide bad situations in beautiful places. The trees kept you on the road, not paint. The road *in* ironically is sometimes actually your way *out*.

The cabin had nothing. No power. No running water. No heat. No air conditioning. No insulation, not even dry wall. A couple bunk rooms, a kitchen, and a common room with a large table and a wood stove. I suppose at that point, though, the way I saw it, it really had everything. Everything I could need then, which wasn't much at all.

It was dark unless you lit the propane lanterns hanging from old nails pounded in the log beams overhead. I didn't like the lanterns; they made a loud hiss and their propane tanks were too industrial and modern. The hiss - one you wouldn't notice back in the real world where life itself was noise - there in the cabin's quiet sounded like a jet flying overhead, like white noise from an out of range radio station. The one you just turn off because silence is better. The hiss was annoying.

I was happy to turn out the lights and go to sleep on the old mattress in my bunk room. Just an old military surplus sleeping bag on a bare mattress, staring up at the bottom of the bare mattress above. When the last light in the cabin was turned off, everything disappeared. Pitch black. The wall to my left and the bunk above were suddenly gone and all that remained was space. If I looked hard eventually my eyes adjusted to the dark, and out the window I could just make out where the tops of the trees ended, and the night sky began. Only because of the stars.

In the absence of man-made noise, I was left to listen to a lonely loon calling to a mate that wasn't there all through the night on Green Lake outside my window. The call of the loon is a true north country experience. It's haunting and beautiful, and in the still of an Adirondack night, its voice pierces the silence like a sharp dagger. Maybe a little more poetic than I usually like to be, but it's the best description I could come up with. It carried for miles in the quiet. There were no answers.

It was depressing to hear the loon calling all night for such a long time. Knowing how great of a distance its calls traveled and not hearing a return confirmed that out there we were truly alone. It wasn't just humans that wished for companionship and couldn't find it; apparently it was a natural thing. It didn't make any pains I felt inside me any less, but it did put things into perspective. The next day the loon was gone.

The lake was very alive. Fish rose sporadically as I stood on the dock and peered out into a lifting fog. It rolled and churned on the surface like something alive. Like the flames of a fire it rose, becoming thinner and wispy as it reached higher until it eventually dissipated into the atmosphere. It moved on the water with no direction.

At first, it seemed as if the entire fog was rotating as a whole; but then as I stood and studied it, I saw that it had no direction at all. Over here it moved towards the center of the lake, over there it moved towards me. In another place it was moving away. Creeping. Never with any speed. It never collided, it simply flowed in every direction at once. It rose like fire, it flowed like liquid, but yet, it was nothing you could touch. I imagined a scientist could relate its movements on the lake to temperature differentials and thermal activity. I took it for what it simply was. Fog. I didn't need to know any more.

As I walked down the primitive wooden steps from the cabin above down to the lake before the sun was completely up, I caught a glimpse of three silhouettes leaving the lily pads along the shore. It looked a little lock-ness-ish, but I knew they were the silhouettes of three otters. Their voices were a hoarse and squishing thing, and the only thing I could compare them to would be someone walking in waterlogged boots. They dove below the surface as soon as they saw me and didn't show themselves again. I wondered how long an otter could stay under. When I was old enough to shoulder a rifle for my country, but still too young to drink, I used to be able to stay under for just over two minutes...but that was a long time ago. Out there in the dark and silence, everything seemed like it was a long time ago, and so far away.

On the first day, the lake was a big mystery to me. Fish rose inconsistently but more than enough to make me think I'd be able to catch one. But this wasn't a bass lake. If it was, I'd have caught something. Bass were easy to find and predict. Toss a popper by the weeds. Toss a popper by the logs. Toss a popper in the middle of the lake sometimes. Bass, they eat.

JP said the fish rising were brook trout and the bigger fish I saw a couple times launching themselves on the far side of the lake were landlocked salmon, but I'd have to take his word for it. I wasn't going to see anything on my line on Green Lake before the end of my stay. Green Lake was merely the way to identify our cabin. It had nothing to do with any fish I caught. Not that I didn't try.

Cruising trout taking something from the surface that you never see on a lake is one of those things that will put an angler in his place, and there on Green Lake I was put in mine. That lake was clear, crystal clear. You needed a really good long cast. On some days I have a poor *short cast*. You needed to be able to make a long cast, with a long leader, and whatever the tiny thing was that the trout were feeding on, and you needed it to lay out and come to rest like a single silk from a spider on a light breeze.

The landing of the fly line spooked everything. The water was so clear I imagined everything that wasn't exactly what they were looking for got closely inspected and ignored. But even before those details, you needed to know where the cruising fish were. A rise here or there on a huge glass surface of liquid was intimidating, to say the least.

On a river, predicting where a fish is was child's play compared to Green Lake. Behind that rock out of the current. Just below those riffles. In that foam line, the eddy along the opposite side. Right there in that run where it keeps consistently rising every forty seconds or so.

The lake was wide, long, and flat. The only structure showing on it was the canoe I made my casts from. How was I supposed to place this #21 trico emerger - something so small that I could barely tie it on - on such a huge, featureless thing, in a place that a twelve-inch fish was going to stumble across it in its random wanderings? When you're trying to make long delicate casts to nowhere in particular and a fish rises within thirty feet of the canoe underneath your back cast, it was hard to believe anything other than the fish were screwing with me. I was the brunt of some fish joke, I just knew it. But I could take it. It sounds cliché, but I was just glad to be there.

On the second day, we fished the river. It was a river we'd all fished before, just never here because it was private. I was excited to fish it just because it wasn't the lake, and it felt good to feel excited about fishing again. Finally.

In the morning after a little breakfast, we took a walk down the trail that traveled away from the lake on the left side of the cabin, to see how far the river was. Me, I don't just take random walks to rivers just to see if they're there. So naturally I carried a fly rod. The trail didn't go far before it came to the river, and when it came into view, it was one of those sights that just makes you feel good inside. There's really no other way to explain it. You were just walking. Then you come to the river. You see that it has a rocky bottom, a long slow stretch upstream, a set of riffles downstream, and some big boulders on the far side in the slack water. The whole thing just looks fishy and suddenly you feel good. You feel *alive*.

There were a couple flat bottom boats upside down and lying in the undergrowth on the bank. On the other side of the river, which was probably about fifty or sixty feet wide, was a trail marker and some type of sign about a boat always being on both sides. Apparently the boats were there only for people to cross the river. I thought it was odd as I waded across. It seemed like it would be more work to flip a boat, put it in, and then fight the current, when you could just wade it.

While I was thinking about it and considering where to cast, I looked back up the bank to see John and JP talking to a guy in running shoes and shorts. It turned out that he was at the club for a wedding and was just out for his morning run, trying to figure out how he was going to get the boat back to the other side on his own. So naturally, I volunteered to pull the boat back across once he was out and on his way again. I was already in the river, anyhow.

He was a nice enough guy, and I watched him trot off into the woods on the other side of the river once he'd paddled across, but I remember thinking to myself that his parents must have been cruel people. He'd introduced himself with a handshake and said his name was Gaylord. I figured it must have been a family name, but nonetheless, he was probably a pretty tough guy in the end for all the beatings he must have taken on the playground as a kid. I figured it was probably kind of like that Johnny Cash song, "A Boy Named Sue." I imagined worse.

JP and John left me there at the river while they walked back to get their fly rods and waders, so of course I began fishing. Standing in the slow water and casting across and downstream, I'd caught a couple little brookies out of the riffles by the time they got back. We waded across the river and picked up the trail where Gaylord had disappeared on his morning run a half hour earlier and headed upstream.

The woods were beautiful that morning; nice and cool, no bugs to bother us yet, a well-marked and beaten path. But while the trail was a matter of convenience, it was an aggravation as well. The trail led us to where we wanted to go, but it seemed to take forever to get there. At the end of our hike was a falls. I just wanted to get there and start casting. I don't think I'd been excited enough to be impatient about actually getting somewhere in months.

About a quarter mile from the falls, we came to a long walking bridge over a tributary stream and it looked pretty promising to me. It flowed down through the woods above us and as it passed under the bridge, it cut its way through tall bushy grass intermixed with saplings. It flowed through this for forty yards before intersecting with another larger stream that I'd call more of a creek, which flowed off to our left and out of sight.

I climbed down from the bridge on a stone pier at its halfway point and lowered myself into the high grass flanking the water. The grass was about thigh deep, good cover. I should've moved through the high grass down to the end where it met the creek and fished upstream, but my impatience got the better of me.

After making a couple casts from the grass, I lowered myself into the water and began making casts downstream. My strategy was that if I made long enough casts downstream, I'd be casting to fish that were facing me but were too far away to have seen me yet. The strategy sounded plausible in my head, but if there were any brookies, they either didn't like my fly or they made me, and the plan was a bust.

Of course, the angler who spooks fish and catches nothing will usually resort to telling you there were no fish there. It's always possible that anglers in this situation don't realize they're scaring off the fish and therefore think that there just weren't any. But of course, it's an easy enough excuse to make, too; that there were just no fish in the stream to catch.

Either way, slowly working my way downstream, flanked by tall grass several feet above my head on both sides of me, finally sparked something inside again. I didn't realize it then, but I hadn't thought about anything but exploring and casting once I'd dropped down from the bridge. The adventure was doing exactly what it was supposed to do. What I'd lost during the last few months had shown back up again. Hope. I was casting and hoping again, finally. I climbed back up the pier and we continued across the bridge, passing back into the woods.

Not long after, we could hear the rumble of the falls and not much after that we finally laid eyes on them. The trail came out on the left banks of the river and looking left we looked up the river at something straight off a post card or out of a travel magazine. I started picking out places to lay out a cast immediately.

John and JP made their way down to a huge boulder that looked like an obvious place to fish from if you'd ever seen one. I moved down stream of them and started stripping a small streamer in all the likely spots. We began catching trout almost immediately. I could've never gone back to the cabin, or back to civilization at all for that matter, and been perfectly happy in this place.

They weren't tall falls; it's not like it was a hundred-foot plunge into roaring white water, but they weren't anything I'd take a canoe over, either. Water crashed down over huge boulders, dropped off tall rock shelves, and on our side the river was funneled into a fast and powerful run along the boulder that JP and John stood on. Out farther, the water wasn't quite as fast, but none of it looked like a smart place to go for a swim.

Across from us on the opposite side climbed a wall of eroded earth; a mix of rock and dirt and the odd dead tree branch that had fallen but not made it all the way to the river, hanging up on some unseen protruding form. It met the river's swift current at its bottom side and high above it met the forest at its roots. Trees stood tall, pines with massive trunks that reached to the sky, seeming even taller than they were because of their position atop the already tall cliff. And above all of them stood a single natural structure. An ivory tower.

It *had been* an ancient tree when it had reached the end of its life, but now it could hardly be called a tree at all. Now it was more of a pole. It stood at the very edge, as if it stood in defiance of the power of the river far below and the years of rain and weather that had eroded away the soil to within inches of its base. And it stood tall, easily another fifteen feet above all the others around it. But it *had been* taller.

An osprey nest sat on its broken off top, and I felt jealousy towards the bird that claimed the highest point overlooking the river. No branches, just a bark-less and white sun-bleached trunk standing in such a place as to have a view of the falls, what lied above them, and the river flowing far downstream. From my days climbing cell towers, I knew that as beautiful as a place like this was standing *in it*, it never compared to the view looking down on it, and at all that it was surrounded by.

An Ornithologist would tell you that an osprey built that nest because they live on a diet of fish, and their nests are always built on the tallest vantage point in the area, and always close to water. But I knew the truth. I'd seen the truth from the osprey's view. An osprey built that nest up there because of the view. It was prime real-estate. It was the penthouse in the skyscraper overlooking Central Park. The river with the fish in it just meant takeout dinner was close by. It was all about the view. I wished I could cross the river, climb the cliff wall, climb the tree, and sit in that nest. Take it all in. Never leave.

We fished the falls for a couple hours. We moved above them, too, and it was a different world up there. The crashing water became dulled, background noise from another place once we were above them. The water was deep, but clear enough to see that the bottom was a scattered mess of boulders. Ranging in size from fairly large to gigantic, they disappeared into the depths as the dark tannin-stained water swallowed them into nothingness. It was the kind of place that stirred your imagination. You could see a fish in every crevice, behind every rock, in the black depths of the narrow run above the boulder-strewn pool above the falls. Your head told you they were there, even if you couldn't see them. They had to be.

It would've been a great place to have a spare spool for the reel with a sink tip line, and maybe even some god-awful split shot, but no one had anything like that. We'd planned on fishing a shallow Adirondack river, not this. The banks were solid granite up here, not boulders or rocks; they were the earth itself. Here, the bank you stood on was *the Planet Earth*. The banks choked the river; they narrowed and came together, but the bottom dropped away terrifically. Quite terrifyingly when you really stood there and studied it.

The river in that one spot was as dark as the sky at night if the stars were all gone, and its current was boiling. Swells of water from below boiled to the top and collided with other boiling currents. There was no noise, no white water. It was simply a scary, deep, and fast-moving force to be reckoned with. I doubted even a spin fisherman with a couple ounces of weight could ever hit the bottom there. The hydraulics in that stretch could probably float lead.

We moved back below the falls and fished there a little while longer. When we were satisfied with the rainbows and brookies we'd caught, it was decided that we should start heading back down river. We weren't going to take the trail back that had gotten us there; it was never part of the plan. We were going to fish our way back down the river. I mean, once you find the river and its fish, how could you ever leave it behind for a trail through the woods?

We spent the next three hours fishing, wading, insulting each other's casts, and generally forgetting all about anything that lied beyond the Adirondacks. I'd even forgotten that we were actually on our way back to a cabin, in all honesty. There was nothing but the river and three friends with fly rods. What more could you really need?

The cabin. It had everything I needed and nothing I didn't, when it came down to it. A lake and a river. Trees and mountains. Loons and deer and moose and bears and otters for neighbors. Nails pounded into the slab wood siding to hang fly rods and waders. A porch to sit on. No power, no running water. No cell phones. No social media, no politics, no war. No divorce, no wife filing for divorce. From this end, the dirt road led out, but to me it was *back in*. I'd have been perfectly happy to wake up the next day to find it all gone, wiped from the earth like a broom brushes away dirt on the porch steps. Out there, I was home. It was like the old saying, *home is where the heart is*. I didn't think I had a heart left after the past few months. Now I knew I still did, because it didn't want to leave. It was at home out there.

14

Hair Cuts

It wasn't that I was trying to make a statement by not cutting my hair, but I hadn't cut it since maybe June, probably close to six months. I simply hadn't cared to. Whiskey and self-loathing had pretty much taken up anytime that could have been allotted to a haircut. And really, the only reason I'd cut it for the past seventeen years was because Holly didn't like it long. I wasn't living to someone else's standards anymore. But I guess even not trying to make a statement ends up making a statement in the end. And if you're lucky, eventually the whiskey runs out.

The long, bushy sideburns exploding from under my ball cap and the unruly hair covering the back of my neck must've made some type of a statement, because everyone at work kept asking when I was going to get a haircut. They weren't coming right out and saying, *"you look like shit,"* but I could tell they were thinking it. I didn't care, which I suppose was the statement being made in the end.

And then *the morning* came. I woke up and realized that wearing a ball cap just wasn't cutting it anymore. I was constantly tucking hair under my hat trying to get it off my ears. And I needed to move on. Move forward. I was going house hunting. But first I needed to clean up a bit.

I hadn't been in a barber shop in probably fifteen years. An electric razor, a number two on the sides and a number three up top had been the extent of my monthly hair maintenance. Why? Well, because I didn't have to do anything to it. Less time combing your hair on an early Saturday morning means faster out the door and faster to the fish. It's simple angling logic. One of my ex-wife's hairdresser friends had always done it because she could keep the back straight.

I walked into the Gentlemen's Corner Barber Shop and found myself sitting in the seat at the far end. A friendly barber in a black apron with brown leather straps named Vic introduced himself in the way that the current and up and coming generations seem to have forgotten or have simply never been taught. A handshake and a smile, Vic moved a little slow and stiff, and told me how it seemed harder and harder to get up out of a chair these days. But once he was up it was all fine. A younger barber walked in and handed him a cupcake and said, *"Happy birthday Vic."* He smiled. I liked Vic. He reminded me of my barber when I was a little kid.

Johnny Harp had a barber shop in West Utica. I can remember going there when everything looked huge to a little boy not even in kindergarten yet, when you looked up at everything and everyone else looked down to you. You know, those times when you thought everything seemed so much bigger but looking back now, you realize that you were just *that small*. It wasn't so much Harp's Barber Shop and the red, white, and blue barber pole outside that I look back so fondly on as the candy store next door and the rope licorice I usually got after a haircut. Johnny usually gave my mother some change for me to get some candy. He wasn't just our barber, he was a friend of the family.

Sometime later, Johnny Harp moved his shop a couple blocks up onto Whitesboro Street, only a block or so from my grandparents' house, and I was allowed to walk to the barber shop on my own as I got a little older. I laugh about that today, because the neighborhood has changed quite a bit. I'd never dream of letting my twelve-year-old walk that street *any time of day*. Things change. Memories remain.

I've always credited my grandfather for my love of fishing. But sitting in Vic's chair as hair fell to the floor all around me, I started to remember Johnny Harp, how he could carry on a conversation with anyone - even a little four-year-old boy - and how I never heard a single bad thing about him. But more importantly, I remembered a specific day.

He pulled up in an old gas guzzling 1970's-something car and lifted a brown metal tackle box and a cane fishing pole out of the trunk. I don't remember what he said, I was preoccupied with doing something in the dirt - probably playing with some toy, a matchbox car or a Star Wars figure, I can only imagine. The car was big and brown, maybe green.

I can see him getting out and walking to the trunk and my father sticking his shovel into the ground and walking over to the car. They talked, I played. When Johnny left, my father brought the tackle box and fishing pole over and set them on the ground. I remember him saying that Johnny said he couldn't fish anymore and that he'd given them to us.

Later at the dinner table, I can still hear my parents talking about Johnny being sick, and probably the first time I ever heard the word *cancer* and it sticking in my head. It didn't mean anything to me. It's quite possible that back in the early 80's cancer wasn't such a common word, but then again I suppose it's also quite possible that it's just like looking back and thinking everything looked bigger back then. When you're a little kid that hasn't learned anything about life yet, looking back things were just very *different.* Like the word *cancer* then compared to when I hear it today. Today you hear it all the time. Everyone gets some form of it. Some ridiculous number, like one in three people.

Sitting in Vic's barber chair brought me back to a time when men were polite and shook hands sealing a deal. They looked you in the eye and told you what they thought. They had pride in what they did and even if they didn't; they knew someone had to do it. They trusted another man to put a straight razor to their face and never thought twice about it.

And when they learned their time was coming, they gathered up their fishing tackle and they gave it to a friend knowing that they had sons, and that fathers are meant to take their sons fishing. As I got older, my brothers and I emptied that tackle box little by little until there was nothing left. The old cane spinning rod stood in a shed corner unused collecting dust. I don't even think I ever realized where it had come from.

Somehow, Johnny's memory had all but escaped my mind by the time I'd hit my high school years. The irony in that is by the time I'd just barely scraped my way through the twelfth grade, my hair reached past my shoulders. Johnny Harp had been gone for a good many years. He wasn't cutting my hair, but he was right there every time I rummaged through that metal box for worm hooks or an old lure.

I bought a house. I'd been looking out in the country but couldn't find anything I could afford. I looked about a half hour north but couldn't find anything that the bank was willing to give me money on. I eventually settled on a house right at the bottom of the street from my boys. The idea of having to see my ex-wife drive by all the time was a hard pill to swallow, especially considering I'd be seeing her in someone else's pick-up truck. It sounded like an old country song to me. The upside was that Jake and Carter could jump on their bikes and be at my house in about a minute. And that was hard to dismiss. Plus, I was just down the street from Chris and Kelly. Not to mention, there was still the creek out back.

While I was moving stuff in, I realized that in the large bunch of old fishing rods I had standing in a corner, I still had Johnny Harp's old cane fishing rod. I hung it on the wall, separate from the others. Likewise, while setting up my collection of old tackle in a display cabinet, I realized that an old red and white wooden fishing lure that looks like it was meant to slightly imitate a swimming mouse silhouette came from that old tan tackle box he'd left with us. It was the only lure to survive me and my two younger brothers' excursions to the pond next door when we were kids. Then I realized I even have the tackle box itself. Today it's packed with excess fly-tying materials.

I didn't think that any of it was supposed to be some kind of sign, or wake-up call to something...nothing like that. But it was good to look back fondly on someone I'd all but forgotten about with sudden vividness.

The world needs more good barbers. And I don't mean the kind that can turn a mop into a fashion statement. I mean the kind that will look you in the eye when they shake your hand, talk to you like an old friend when you're in their chair, and give a little kid their tackle box when they find it's their time to move on from this world.

15

You can't Catch Fish with Lawn Mowers

I thought I was being clever when I bought my lawn mower. My lawn is small, really small. It's one of the reasons I settled on the house. I could probably get away with cutting it with a long pair of scissors and raking the clippings into a zip lock bag, if I were the kind of person that thinks grass clippings should be bagged and disposed of. But I'm not. I absolutely hate mowing the lawn. So, when I bought the mower, I felt so smart.

I wasn't going to pay for a self-propelled push mower for so little square footage, and then I considered that gas-powered push mowers that aren't self-propelled aren't the easiest things to push. So why even spend the money on a gas mower at all? If I was going to have to push it, why should I have to put gas in it? I bought one of those old-school reel mowers for seventy bucks. Pushes no harder than a gas push mower but doesn't use the gas.

I felt like a genius once I really started to analyze the situation. It was quiet, which meant that I could mow early in the morning or later in the evening without waking up the neighbors, without being *that guy* in the neighborhood. And not needing to mow during the day meant that while everyone else was mowing, I could be fishing. I could flip on my front porch light and mow by the dull yellow light and the illumination of the street light on the corner, while fishing all day. So far I'd carried out half of the strategy. I'd fished all day. I had yet to mow at night. Or early in the morning, for that matter.

Besides being close to my boys, there was one other reason I bought this house. It had been vacant for about two years. The lawn was never mowed, so I figured everyone had gotten used to it and I might not get the stink eye from the neighbors. What better place could I find close to my boys than a house with a creek behind it and neighbors who'd gotten used to a lawn that was never mowed?

I hadn't gotten too many dirty looks yet, but while I was stringing up my fly rod on the front porch one day, the guy across the street did walk over to introduce himself and welcome me to the neighborhood. Joe's a real nice guy. So nice, in fact, that out of the blue while eyeing the streamers stuck in my baseball cap, he offered me a free lawn mower that he said he didn't use anymore. What a nice guy. I asked him if he fished much and he said no. He didn't have much time. Always working around the house.

Coincidentally, the fishing had picked up in the creek over the past month. The last weekend, Jake and Carter had wanted to fish both days, and who was I to tell them, *"Sorry but I can't right now, I have to mow the lawn."* I was trying to set a good example, trying to be a good dad. Telling them I was too busy to take them fishing was, as far as I'm concerned, an absolute tragedy each time an opportunity is missed. When I'm on my death bed, I don't plan on reminiscing about how perfect the grass was. I plan on telling about how every time Carter would hook a decent fish when he was a young boy that he'd always turn and look at me with disappointment on his face and tell me, *"I'm snagged on something,"* and gesture to me to take the rod and unsnag it. Only for me to feel the rod shudder and hand it back to him in hilarious excitement, *"You're not snagged, it's a fish. Reel!"*

The week before, one afternoon after I'd gotten home from work and they'd gotten home from school, they asked if we could go fishing. I heard a mower running a few houses up and looked at my lawn. I didn't really care what it looked like, so I told them to get their old sneakers on while I got their spinning rods out of the garage.

They put their wading sneakers on and then grabbed their baseball gloves and patiently played catch in grass half way to their knees while I strung up my 6wt. I plucked a couple streamers from the dash of the Jeep and stuck them in my hat, then we walked out back using the dirt road to the Little League field to get to the creek. Our shadows, two boys and their father with fishing rods, kind of felt a little Mayberry-ish. I liked it.

When we got to the creek, they stood in ankle deep water and cast their marabou jigs to the shade on the far side, targeting the deeper and darker holes and trenches. I set my fly rod down to watch them and never made a single cast for the next two hours.

They had spaced themselves apart enough to not cast over the other's line, but close enough to carry on some of the most casual and entertaining conversations you'd ever hear between and eight-year-old and a thirteen-year-old. They talked about everything from last year's Little League season to fishing for bass down on the farm in Cobleskill to what they thought was going to happen in the next "Ant Man" movie. They sounded like two old friends out fishing. *Exactly* the way it's supposed to be.

When they would move, they'd offer to hold the other's fishing pole as they climbed over fallen trees or up a slippery bank, and they never once got mad or argued. They were two brothers, two sons, every now and then needing a dad to get a jig out of a tree branch or off a rock on the bottom. My fly rod stayed standing against trees or lying back in the tall grass the entire time, while I stood in the background and observed a perfect afternoon. I became part of the story only when the net was needed, a handful of times at most.

A couple days later, on a Saturday, the lawn a couple inches higher, we were on the creek again; but this time I rigged up a fly rod and actually fished. It's really something to realize that suddenly you're making casts, and so are your boys, and you're not helping them at all. It's not a dad helping and showing his two sons how to fish…it's a dad *fishing with his two sons*. I hooked into a decent smallmouth and *Carter* netted it for *me*.

One night we had a Little League game, otherwise I guarantee you that we'd have been out back fishing. The lawn was really tall. It was like night and day, my disaster of a yard compared to the freshly cut lawn of my neighbors butting up to it. It kind of looked like a scaled down version of a field that ends where a forest begins. The sun was coming up early enough now that I could probably cut it for the third time of year in the morning with that quiet little reel mower before work. But, the sun was coming up early enough now that I could probably get an hour of fishing in on the creek before work. There just weren't enough hours in the day.

16
All Things Fly Fishing

It was innocent enough. The Little League field is right out back behind my house. It's conveniently positioned between my back door and the creek, the two places we seem to spend most of our time between spring and fall. I was walking Carter to the field entrance for a Saturday morning of fall ball, and we only had to pass my neighbor's house on the left before we'd be through the gate and the sounds of kids and baseballs smacking leather gloves would take over the rest of the morning. But I suppose *most* things happen innocently enough. It's how a lot of things start really…innocently enough.

As we walked past the neighbor's house, we saw the garage sale set up. My eyes automatically scanned the few tables and odds and ends as we walked by. It was harmless, but subconsciously my mind will tell my eyes to scan for anything fishing related the way airport security looks for specific shapes in the X-rays.

At first, my eyes caught sight of what I thought was a nice wooden bookshelf. My collection of books on anything to do with fishing had filled the one bookshelf I owned, and I'd been thinking of adding another in the living room. You can never have enough books on fishing, but you *can have* too little shelf space for them. But on closer inspection, it wasn't a bookshelf at all, it was a nice wooden gun cabinet. I didn't need a gun cabinet, I needed a bookshelf. So my eyes kept searching as we passed by.

Then they fell on the card table closest to the open garage. I suggested to Carter that we cut through the garage sale to get to the baseball field gate. The suggestion may or may not have been motivated by the table full of old fishing rods surrounded by a small pile of tackle boxes. This is where *innocently enough* turns into *intent*. I got a good look at the table; my neighbor saw me looking and he told me if there was something I wanted he'd hold it for me until after the game. I told him I'd be back in five minutes. The game wouldn't start for another half hour.

I ended up walking Carter to the field, then running back home, driving the Jeep over to the gas station to get money out of the ATM, and adding two more fly rods and an old rod tube with several old and disheveled bamboo rod tips inside it to an already obnoxious tangle of antique fishing rods of both the spin and fly-fishing genres. Honestly, I use the word "antique" for two reasons. For one, yes, they all range in age from fairly old to pretty old. But for the other, well, antique sounds a lot more sophisticated than a bunch of old worthless rods that no one threw out even though they're too old and ratty to use.

They *were cool.* I'm not saying I just bought old fly rods and a handful of bamboo tips simply because they were in front of me. For instance, one of the fly rods was an old metal Horrocks-Ibbotson. They were cheap rods back in their days, common rods for the common blue-collar sports, and they were made in Utica, N.Y. And Utica is only about an eight-minute drive from my house.

I was born in a hospital in Utica. My parents were both from Utica. Utica is that city around here that when you travel to somewhere else and people ask you where you're from, you don't tell them the name of your little village because they probably won't know it. You say Utica. Of course, the company is gone now like most companies from a lost era. So, I had to buy the rod. It was cool.

Utica was a huge industrial city when the country was in it's heyday of manufacturing. When the best stuff said M*ade in U.S.A.* on it and people were proud of that label - a little of everything was made right here in Utica. And Horrocks-Ibbotson Co. called it home. I don't ever remember it, even at forty-three years old I can still say I'm too young. But anyone who's still around to remember the old days around here will tell you that there wasn't a fisherman alive locally that didn't have H-I fishing gear in their closet in one respect or another. But it wasn't just local; it was distributed all over the country to sporting goods and department stores, a common house hold name.

I was lucky enough to end up with my great-grandfather's tackle boxes on my mother's side after my grandfather passed away. I've kept them the way they were when we first opened them, like two rusty time capsules. But before putting everything back in the way we found it, I inspected lures and gear for names and such. In general, I just got a big thrill out of inspecting the tackle of my great-grandfather from Indiana, a man I had never met. In it there was an ancient looking plastic reel spooled with equally as ancient looking fly line. I found the model embossed on the back side, it read *Vernley Trout Reel, Horrocks-Ibbotson Co. Utica, N.Y.*

At first I just thought it was cool to come across an old *trout reel* made in Utica. But then it hit me - because I have a fondness for local history - that it was my own proof without hearing it from another local old timer. Good stuff, indeed, did once go on in the city. My great-grandfather lived in Indiana, not N.Y. Yet here was his old tackle box, probably last fished in the late forties or early fifties, with a fly reel in it from right here. The reel had been made here then shipped to Indiana. It was most likely sold in the quintessential mom and pop sporting goods store or something more like a Sears and Roebuck type department store back in his day, and then fished who-knows-where. And then it ended up back here in N.Y. In my hands.

I used to grab old fishing gear when I saw it for cheap, and sneak it into my writing room quietly when I was married. But after buying my house, I began to actively seek it out. I didn't even make a conscious effort of it, it just started to happen naturally. It was like people I didn't even know new I'd just gotten divorced somehow and started flashing old reels and worthless fly rods and anything that remotely had to do with fishing at me like a guy opening his jacket and flashing twenty-something gold watches on a street corner. *Hey, bub, you know what time it is? You need a watch, pal? Take a look here.* And I'd be bringing home more old fishing stuff. Rods, reels, framed paintings by amateurs who obviously loved fly fishing but weren't the greatest artists. I bought a painting in a bulk load of fishing stuff one day and I swear, it's old, a little faded, but the trout looks cross-eyed to me. I'm not sure I'd know how to paint a cross-eyed fish, but I bought one *because there was no one to tell me no.*

That type of thing went on for months. Before the divorce, I had one little room in my house that I'd stuffed with all my fishing paraphernalia. Now I had my own house. *A whole house*. I bought a small house because I didn't need much room. So what did I do? Filled it with everything and anything that would follow me home that had something – anything - to do with fishing. I thought the worst thing about a divorce was the divorce. One day, I came to my senses and realized that the divorce was still the worst thing, but a close second now was not having anyone to threaten me with a divorce if I brought more old fishing junk home.

I had four corners in my living room, but I had old rods standing upright in five. A narrow shelf above my coat rack in the kitchen spanned the length of the wall. When I filled it with old whiskey bottles shaped like fish, I went and acquired a corner shelf from Chris's garage and stuck it in the dining room so that I'd have more room for the other fishing-themed whiskey bottles that wouldn't fit in the kitchen.

I hadn't come across an old fly reel that I didn't like. And by *like*, I mean *bring home*. Don't even ask about the curio cabinet full of ancient rotten wooden lures and bait caster reels full of old black nylon line. And yeah, those two Wheatley fly boxes full of old flies hanging over my writing desk? I found them in two large cardboard boxes full of *"stuff"* ranging in anything from an old Florida fly fishing club patch to some old and musty rooster capes that I had to throw out after exhuming them from their resting places in the bottom of the boxes. Those were honestly part of one of my cooler hauls.

Someone contacted me through Facebook to take advantage of my weak constitution when it came to all things fly fishing. They sent me photos of an antique ten drawer chest full of all kinds of old flies and stuff. It was nothing anyone *needs,* but then again no one *needs* to do heroine, either; yet they still do it, even though everyone knows that heroine first ruins your life, then kills you. Compared to heroine, the chest seemed a better choice.

When I made the forty-five-minute drive to go check it out, I found it to be an old piece out of a store of some kind. Probably a fly shop or tackle shop by the looks of it. It would've been placed on a counter with drawers facing the clerk and the back facing the customer. On the back were a few catalog pages displayed behind glass so that a customer could look over the fly selection and tell the clerk which numbers they wanted. Across the ornamental wooded trim on top was painted *"Herter's Flies."* Yet another bygone company that supplied sportsman in a bygone era.

But I'll admit that I'm rather attached to the *"Herter's Flies"* store counter cabinet full of everything from old salmon flies to gut leaders still in the original packaging. I used it as kind of an end table by the couch. I can imagine anglers walking up to the counter and studying the black and white pictures of all the different flies and asking for half a dozen *Quill Gordons* or three *Pink Ladies* and three *Silver Doctors,* please. I didn't need it until I saw it, along with the couple boxes of *"one man's junk is another man's treasure."* But now, I couldn't imagine setting my hand-painted salmon fly candy dish, my raggedy mascot, a mounted rooster named Bitchface Malone, or swordfish bottle opener on anything else.

I hung the nicest rods I've acquired above the bookshelf to display them. The only problem with that is that they took up wall space. Wall space I could've used to hang the myriad old paintings and posters of trout and pike and fishing scenes of old men in funny hats fighting mystical fish on mountain streams in cracked and fragile frames.

But probably the coolest thing to come home with me was

right about at the end of it all, when I finally told myself to gain some composure and find some self-respect. Just say no. There was no more room in the house. But I did still have a front porch with nothing but a three-foot-long Rapala lure complete with real treble hooks the likes of which the old Adam West Batman could probably tie on to a rope and scale a building.

My buddy, Dale Coria, sent me a text one day. "Come see me, I have something for your new house. I want you to have it. I think it would be perfect." I called him back and he told me about an old church pew that he had. His wife liked it, but it was always buried under coats and boots in a back room, so they decided it was better off somewhere it would be appreciated. And they'd free up eight feet.

So I drove up the street, picked up Chris, and we took a ride to Dale's house. While we awkwardly raised it above our heads and loaded the eight-foot-long solid oak church pew on the roof, we laughed about the sight it was going to make. We did get a few sideways glances and stares from other cars in traffic, but it wasn't surprising. It's not every day you see a church pew strapped down to a roof rack on a Jeep.

Dale wasn't home when we'd picked it up, so later that night he called me and told me the story of how he'd gotten it. Quite a few years ago, a woman from around here was in New York City and saw a church being gutted. She asked about the pews and ended up buying several. They were over a hundred years old. Years later, Dale had been working on her house and ended up with one of the pews as a partial payment for the work he was doing. I think Dale is the only person I've ever known to work for such a payment. I also think he's the only person that would've thought that I needed a church pew on my porch to begin with.

That following weekend I had Jake and Carter. We were just starting to feel out how this whole *staying at Dad's new house every other weekend thing* was going to work, and we decided to go fishing out back. Normally I'd string up my fly rod on the end of the porch and we'd all change into our old sneakers for the creek in the driveway. But on that weekend, more than once, the boys sat on the pew next to the front door of their dad's new house. It didn't even look odd. If there's one place a church pew can look right at home outside of a church, then it's on a front porch with two boys sitting on it tying their shoes, fishing poles leaning against one end.

I don't go to church. I hadn't thought much of having any faith in quite a long time. *If* God was real, then the place I felt closest to Him was on the creek with a fly rod in my hand. In that respect, it seemed perfectly logical that someone would prepare to go fly fishing by first sitting in a church pew to pull on waders and check the contents of their fly box one last time.

I collected all that old fishing stuff. Filled the house with it. I never considered a church pew as having anything to do with fishing so, of course, I never went looking for one. Now I couldn't imagine getting ready to go fishing without one. Likewise, I couldn't imagine coming back to the house without having the pew to sit in and pull off waders, set down my net and fly box, and lean back with my feet up on the porch rail where I think about the water I was just standing in and everything that I saw.

No one told me not to, so I ended up with a house full of old crap. I told Jake while we sat and ate dinner one night that maybe I'd have a garage sale the next spring and it'd be full of all the old fishing stuff cluttering up the house. He laughed at me; told me I'd just end up buying it back at other garage sales. I almost asked him if he thought he was a real wise guy. Then I bit my tongue because I realized he was probably right, and instead I asked him to pass the fishing bobber salt shaker.

17

Black Flies and Lost Boys

The small farm lake belonging to distant cousins that my grandfather and I fished my entire childhood has always been what I referred to as my *sacred waters*. You know, I have a connection to it that no other waters could ever take the place of. It's in my blood. Sometimes in my dreams. I've written about it numerous times, and outside of my family, I've only ever taken a couple close friends to it. It's sacred for the memories it holds, not the largemouth bass or the bluegills. They're only fish. Merely the reasons for the trips that create the memories.

I've found plenty of great waters since. Waters that I'll plainly admit have better views and scenery, and possibly better fishing on the right day, but nothing I'd ever call sacred. I always thought there could only be one of those. Then we fought our way through an ancient forest in search of a stream, and at forty-one years old, I found a second sacred water...

Three canoes paddled across an Adirondack lake on a fairly calm day. The *Lost Boys,* Tim Bonaparte and Jimi Radisi, paddled the lead boat. They'd earned their title by bush-whacking into this very stream, and I'd been a little envious of them since the first time they'd pushed off in a canoe on their original search nearly a year earlier. I'd planted the idea of them leading us back out into no man's land the night before for a couple reasons. First, it had been eating at me for a year now that I hadn't seen this "*lost stream.*" It was a place I thought about too often for one I'd never seen with my own eyes. And second, I was writing a book that included their grueling excursion, and I felt I just couldn't write about it honestly from only someone else's account. I had to see it - experience it - myself.

The two other canoes consisted of myself and Keith Tidball,

another friend who'd volunteered to come along because he's a kindred spirit - one of those people with a fondness to march off into the remote and unknown - and finally Andrew O'Neil and Dominic, a couple of young film makers who'd driven all the way from Wyoming for the second time to accompany us on our searches for wild, and possibly native, undiscovered Adirondack brook trout.

Friday had been overcast with spotty rain, and we'd already fished two different rivers - one by canoes, the other wading pocket water. But on Saturday, the skies were a bright blue, the tops of evergreens stabbing upward like jagged spears out of the surrounding forest. We aimed the boats at a beach on the far end of the lake with a backdrop of rolling mountains blanketed in a mix of pines and hardwoods. Water swirled after our paddles at the sides of the aluminum canoes.

The only clouds were the blackflies hovering around us; unrelenting, never ceasing. Vicious, maddening clouds...even out here in the middle of the lake. I wore long pants and sleeves, and my buff was doused in enough Deet to probably send an oncologist into cardiac arrest. I had my hat pulled down tight to the top of my sunglasses, but they still constantly bounced around behind the lenses; and you either just got used to them and ignored it, or eventually went insane. I was waiting to see someone throw a paddle to the side and leap into the lake, but it never happened.

We beached the canoes and geared up with short 2wt and 3wt fly rods, fly boxes, water, and a little hope and excitement. And then Tim and Jimi led us down the beach to a foot path that could've easily been mistaken for a game trail or missed altogether if you weren't looking for it. We picked our way single file through a forest of white pines, some of which were close to the biggest I'd ever seen, others seemed obviously second growth.

The ground was a blanket of moss covering absolutely everything...dirt, rock, and hundreds of fallen and rotting trees and branches. Picking our footing carefully meant deciding where to place your next step, whether it be in a soggy patch of moss covering the soaked soil of a low depression, or the decomposing carcass of a fallen pine tree that crisscrossed over another. Sometimes there were several piled like some forgotten battlefield full of the dead; the carnage a mix of the damages left by time and human factors (namely logging, acid rain, and high winds). And then it only got worse.

The pines continued. The piles of deadfalls grew higher and thicker. And then the new growth - the next generation of the evergreen kingdom - crowded in about chest high, growing out of their fallen elders, covering the ground and not only masking ankle twisters and knee poppers, but grabbing fly rods and leaders too. The new growth was doing their best, as much as any child could do, to try and stop the progress of six grown men determined to conquer Mother Nature and find her most prized treasures.

And then the elevation began to drop. We slowly waded through chaos, sometimes shuffling sideways or backing up and going around...downhill. Tim said it was just ahead, and that the real work was about to show itself. I grinned behind my Deet-soaked buff.

The stream's last defense was the thick alders that lined it; so thick that I doubt thorn bushes could've done much better at all to keep us out. The Lost Boys had told me, *"No waders, you'll destroy them in there in two minutes."* I left my waders behind but questioned it, of course. But now I could see; I could confirm.

Pushing though the undergrowth, I felt a stinging on the back of my left calf, and then the same on my right thigh as alder branches that were intertwined better than the fibers in a rope, held me back as I tried to push through. They grabbed fly rods, slashed at faces, pulled hats from heads, but in the end the will of the fly fishermen was more than they could hold back, and we stood in them at the water's edge.

But that didn't mean much, reaching the stream. The struggle continued. The stream, indeed, was a continuous flow of water as all streams are, but it wouldn't give up its precious brook trout easily. As the forest had fought to keep us from the stream, the *stream* would now fight to keep us from the *fish*. Where the alders flanked the stream, crowding it so that the only means of a cast would be a roll cast or bow and arrow cast at best, the stream itself was nothing more than open water here and there broken up by chaotic and frustrating log jams. Luckily, it wasn't more than ten feet wide or less, bow and arrow casts and the occasional roll cast were all that was needed for the most part.

For every ten-foot stretch of open water there was another ten of log jam or deadfalls above and below it. And where the water was open, the trees overhung so much that a cast without a snag was more of a surprise than the fish we began to see. They flashed up at our flies out of the tannin-stained dark shadows, sometimes every cast, sometimes every other. But every log jam, every sunken log, and every clump of slimy undulating weeds seemed to hide more brook trout.

Trout were rocketing out from their hiding spots in the log jams and from behind rocks on the sandy bottom, or from under sunken pine tree tops that had long ago been snapped from the trees by winds and cast down into the stream to become more structure to conceal its most prized possessions. The more I saw of this, the more I witnessed and observed, and the less I noticed of the struggle of the fishing itself. It became easy because it was just what it took.

The alders and the mushy moss-covered ground, the piles of dead falls and the masses of log jams all in such close quarters, the black flies bouncing around behind my sunglass lenses - they became background, white noise if you will, to the fact that this stream was indeed the birthplace, a sheltered nursery, to a watershed full of the same fish. All wild, all natural, native. Their DNA never having been influenced by *hatchery fish*. The same as it was at the last ice age. The importance of this place hit me like the proverbial *ton of bricks*, and I knew right then I'd never look at the entire watershed the same ever again. Without this little stream, these fish might not have ever survived human kind.

    I may not have had a lifetime's stockpile of memories like I did with the farm lake, but after one trip in to a little brook winding its way through some of the densest and unnavigable land I'd ever pushed through (and after seeing wild, native, heritage strain trout in numbers I'd hardly believe without seeing them myself in waters most any anglers I know wouldn't ever bother with for such *little trout*) I'd found my second sacred waters.

18

Western NY Speculations

There are some stories that I have a more difficult time deciding where to start than others. Some come pretty obvious to me. "I got up, got dressed, and with a fly rod in hand, I headed out to the Jeep and pointed it north." That's always a simple but effective beginning. Or "It was -15 outside and the creek was frozen over solid, so I clamped a hook in the vice to pass the time between now and the next thaw..." Some stories are just that easy to start.

I'm not really sure where to start this one. I could start it by telling how the previous year - around this time, more or less - I was supposed to drive west, taking a three-day weekend to rent a small cabin in the Finger Lakes from an angler I'd never met in person yet. I'd actually only known him as a profile on Facebook and Instagram. He seemed like a decent guy and it'd been a slow winter. So I took Steve Firlit up on his offer of a cabin and directions to fish the Cohocton River nearby.

Only a couple days before I was supposed to drive out there, the state was buried under a snow storm and the trip was called off. Here in Upstate N.Y., we don't stop fishing just because it's winter, but that storm dumped over three feet on us in hours. Mother Nature reminds you how small you are every now and then. So I never made the trip and we never met in person.

Now (a year later) here I was talking to him, finally in person, at the Fly Fisher's Workshop at the Brighton's Twelve Corners Middle School in Rochester. I was sitting behind a folding table and hocking my book, hoping to sell enough to at least pay for my gas money for the weekend, and we were laying out a loose plan for fishing the next day before I made the two-and-a-half-hour drive back home.

I could start it there, or I could start it in another place...

The 16 Stone Brew Pub in Holland Patent. I'd picked it as my hiding spot for a few reasons. First and foremost, my cousins owned it. If I was going to throw money at alcohol, I was going to at least throw it at family. Secondly and probably more importantly, no one besides my cousins knew me up there. And I was looking to be invisible. And they brewed good beer, so there was that.

The idea was that I'd been going through too many whiskey bottles during the divorce, but I was smart enough still to know that if I went someplace to drink and had to drive home, *I wouldn't get drunk*. I was going to a bar...*to not get drunk*. My own logic baffles me sometimes, but this was *actually working*. If I stayed home, I'd go to sleep with the room spinning and have a headache the next day. If I went up to the bar, I'd have two beers - three at the most over four or five hours, give or take - knowing I had to drive. While the strategy worked by me not drowning my sorrows in whiskey every single night, it began to fail at the invisible part.

At some point along the way, I found myself being greeted by the rest of the regulars when I walked in, kind of like *Cheers*. It did feel good though, walking in to smiles and waves. It was good to be greeted by people who were just saying hello because I was there, and not wondering what they were thinking about my failed marriage behind my back. No one knew me up there before the divorce. It was a little more comfortable than the bar in town that was within walking distance. The one where all the locals either knew or wanted to know everyone's business.

I tried to sit quietly and stare at the television above the bar and the football or hockey I cared nothing about, and to ignore the pretty young woman named Nikki, who would always show up and sit a few seats away. But in the end we struck up a conversation. Now here she was, a couple months later, sitting behind my folding table with me as I tried to *not be a salesman*, while I tried to sell my book at the "Fly Fisher's Workshop" in a school building in Rochester.

Like that deep sunk hook in your shoulder that you never saw coming from your back cast, some things *just happen*. Of course, this was much better than a barbed 4/0 hook disguised in feathers and fur stuck fast into the meat of my right arm. But all the same, I never saw it coming and now I was just rolling with it. It was good to feel alive again anyhow...

Or, I could just start this story at the Fly Fisher's Workshop...

It was good. To be set up and sitting behind the table with my books stacked in front of me. To be talking fly fishing with total strangers because that's why we were all there. For one thing, the Jeep had made the two-and-a-half-hour drive flawlessly. The afternoon before, I'd leaned in over the radiator and changed out the thermostat as snow was falling, the thermometer reading a chilly fifteen degrees as my fingers stung from contact with the cold metal wrenches, my skin wet with antifreeze.

Fun Fact: While antifreeze does indeed keep the coolant in your car from freezing during the winter, it in no way has any anti-freezing qualities when your hands are covered in it while outside when it's fifteen degrees.

But now I was standing and talking to Steve Firlit about fishing the next day before Nikki and I headed back towards Utica. The prospect of fly rods and streamers and small streams with lake run fish was more than enough to lift my spirits after a slow winter. I'd only fished once in the past month. I was more than ready.

Across from my table was a young man with dirty blonde dreadlocks - that's the color, not that he needed a shower or anything, by the way - sitting at a vice, tying up some of the best streamers I'd seen in a long time. I'm a streamer junkie, so naturally I was intrigued. At a couple slow points during the day, I stood at his table and learned a little about him, just enough to be jealous. Elvy Foster was twenty-two. He'd been fly fishing and tying since he was twelve and was living life on his own terms.

Guiding, tying, selling fly fishing and tying gear. His streamers were the best I'd seen in a long time.

At forty-two years old, I was looking at this twenty-two-year-old "kid" as someone who had life by the balls whether he realized it or not. They say the grass is always greener on the other side, or as I like to say, the water always looks fishier on the other side of the river.

I looked over at him talking to anglers while he tied at his vice and saw the greener grass, the fishier water. But then I remembered the nature of the sayings and wondered for the rest of the day how green my grass was and if I could find greener, or if it was even worth the risk at this point this late in life. Green grass needs to be mowed after all, and I hate mowing the lawn. Takes time away from fishing.

I left the show with one of Elvy's streamers in my hat and having sold just enough books to pay for my vender's spot and my gas and hotel, *more or less*. It's about all I ever hope to make at most of them, really. People love to talk fishing. And they don't mind picking up a book to look at the cover or flip to the back to somehow figure out if what's inside will keep their attention or not, either. It's as if scanning across a few words will answer that for them. But they don't care to actually buy them very often.

I liken it to picking up a fly rod and holding it out and giving it a few wiggles. As if doing such a thing will tell you how it's going to cast. Let's face it, they're all noodles; whether they're stiff noodles or weak noodles, it doesn't really matter until you have a fly line loading it up on the cast. That's the only time you can really know if it's a rod that fits your style of fishing or not, or if it's really worth the money.

Of course, I've known a couple anglers that could tie a fly line to the end of an *actual broomstick* and cast a dry fly, but that doesn't matter a whole lot. My point is, people love to pick a book up and somehow, by judging its weight or the photo on the back, decide if they'd like to read it or not. And most of the time it's "*not.*" It doesn't really bother me too much. Expect little, be let down less.

More importantly are the people I meet at these things. I can tell you that the fly-fishing culture is alive and well, much bigger in western N.Y. than it is over in my part of the state; and because I took the drive two and a half hours west, I finally got to shake hands with quite a few names that were previously only profiles on social media. My load of books was slightly lighter leaving, but I ended up with a Streamwalker Nets sweatshirt to hold me over while Leif Mermagen crafted my small brookie net for me, and a new book by another author set up at the show, <u>An Affair with Mother Nature</u> by JW Trout.

When I find books on fly fishing, especially collections of stories, they go home with me. There are never enough fish stories. There's also never enough shelf space on my bookcase anymore. It's a disease all to itself, the books. Kind of like the disease of tying flies. You don't need anymore, but you just sit down to the vice and whip up a few more flies because it's there and you don't have anything else to do except mow the lawn. And mowing the lawn sucks when you could be tying flies or reading fishing stories. The only thing to trump them, of course, would be the actual act of fly fishing. But that should go without saying.

As far as my pile of books goes...let's face it, the whole reason we go fishing to begin with is the stories. I mean, you're going out to chase fish, don't get me wrong, but a good day on the water relived later is the motivation for the next trip out, and so on it goes. It's the stories that keep us going back out whether we all realize it or not.

The next morning, Nikki and I met Steve at a park about fifteen miles away, and I rigged up the 7wt for her, while for myself I rigged up a 6wt. She'd never been fly fishing before, and while I thought it was great to be introducing someone new to what had now taken over everything else in my life, I explained that this was a tough place to learn because of the confined small stream with all of the overhanging trees, the undercut banks full of tree branches and roots, and the almost crystal clear water in between such narrow high banks in which large, smart and warry trout were wintering.

I added that learning in the winter was just harder in general. You probably couldn't pick a worse time to take up fly fishing, other than a hurricane maybe. Or a lightning storm, I suppose. The fish aren't moving much, but more so it's usually so cold that you aren't either. Everything is just harder when you're trudging through snow and your fingers are cold enough to have delayed reactions to what your mind tells them to do.

Steve had wandered around a bend, and I'd given Nikki her first lesson the best I could on casting in such a place, when I saw a hair pin turn in the stream to our right and thought it would be a good place to explain how to approach such a spot without spooking fish. Branches reached down from the trees above, ready to grab fly line and leaders, so I demonstrated the side arm cast to keep everything low beneath the cover. I made a cast up into the top of the bend.

As I stripped my streamer back along the far side, a trout - as clear and obvious as watching something happen through a freshly washed window - emerged from the darkness of the undercut bank across and upstream. It was facing upstream and came out of the dark bent like a horseshoe, or like a snake turning to face you when you've walked up behind it. It followed the streamer, inches behind it, its mouth half open as if it just wasn't sure if it was hungry enough to eat or not. It turned away and retreated back under the bank almost even with me, and I finally breathed.

"Did you see it!? Did you see the fish!?" I had polarized sunglasses on, but Nikki didn't so she wasn't sure if she saw it or not. I stripped it past the bank another time but nothing. I figured that was my one and only shot. I should've just let her step up and take my place, but at the very second I thought it, just downstream of where it had gone back under the bank, there it was...the beautiful trout, right in the middle of the stream.

The water was so clear and the stream so narrow, I could make out its spots almost as well as if it were in my hands a foot away from my face. If I had Nikki trade places with me, the movements would have had the fish going for cover, so I dead drifted the streamer to it. This time, the fish backpedaled for about a foot, keeping the hook and faux fur just in front of it, until just before making contact it turned and calmly moved over, letting it pass by. I should have just let Nikki step up and take my place at that point, once again.

But I didn't want to move. The trout was still there. One step to move to a crouching position, to back up into the brush, any movement with such clear water conditions could send the trout retreating up or down stream. Gone but never forgotten. I simply made one more cast, a dead drift with a couple twitches to correct its course to bring it closer. This time the fish ate.

I felt excitement at first. The bend in the 6wt, it had been too long. Steve appeared out of the brush suddenly to see me stepping into the stream. *"You've got a fish on!?"* It was great to feel alive. Finally. Alive in the moment. The trout was gorgeous, and without a measurement I can say *possibly* my biggest. If it was a twenty-two-inch fish we'll call it twenty-three for the sake of embellishment, which is what all anglers get caught up in at one point or another, no matter how honest of a person they may be.

The rest of the day was spent fishing upstream, Steve telling us stories about what the stream was like at different times through the year, and me getting Nikki casting to likely spots. She was awkward in the neoprene waders I'd brought for her, which I expected. *No one* likes the one-piece neoprene wader/boot combos. They're heavy and clumsy, but I thought it was more important for her to be warm on her first time out than anything else. One freezing miserable first experience on the water is all it takes to give someone the impression that it's not for them. Warm and skunked beats cold and skunked any day.

Winter or not, attempting to learn to fly fish for the first time is actually easier on a stream such as the one Steve had brought us to. It was narrow, which meant casting wasn't as big of a deal as it could have been. All I had to do was get Nikki to cast twenty feet and even if she wasn't catching anything, she could reach what she needed to so that she could see that there was at least hope in each cast, if nothing else. It was nothing like needing to cast fifty feet on a big river but only being able to cast twenty. She could reach the other side, and that put a smile on her face.

Probably the best part of the day was when we found fish rising. At the high point of the day our breath wasn't showing in front of our faces anymore and it was pretty nice out. The sun was bright, there was no wind, and it had gotten downright pleasant. As the three of us stood stream side taking a break and having a conversation about how many fish would be stacked up in the stream during the big runs of fall, I thought I saw something. When I saw the questioning look on Steve's face as he studied the same water, I knew I had.

Sure enough, under a small overhanging tree branch and only a foot below where water poured over a log, there was a fish rising regularly to something we couldn't see. There were no bugs in the air, none on the surface that we could see, so I assumed emerging midges. It always seems a good answer when there's nothing to be seen. But then looking at the snow around our feet we spotted tiny black bodies, the smallest black stoneflies I'd ever seen. When you really looked, they were everywhere.

Somehow I had a pattern closely resembling the hatch, so I tied it on. I snuck close enough to reach the rising fish with a delicate cast, explained to Nikki what was happening and what we were about to do, and then laid out the worst cast of the year, slapping the water and spooking the fish. We never saw it again. So I told her that was a lesson in what not to do and we moved on. You can't win them all, especially when you're being watched.

The closest we came to seeing another trout was when Steve was hidden in the brush on a tiny island in the middle of the little stream, casting downstream and swimming a small streamer back upstream, letting it dance and dart in and out underneath a pile of blowdowns. There were a couple flashes and at one point a good but very temporary bend in his rod, and after realizing that more and more casts simply wasn't the answer anymore, we headed back to the parking lot.

Steve and I both agreed that we needed to do it again sometime. It's one of those things we all say that goes without saying, but we say it anyway. It turned out that he had family in Utica, so it was very likely that I'd get to take him out on one of my streams in the future to pay him back. After pulling waders off and breaking down rods we shook hands and said our good byes, new friends that felt like old friends, the way it always is after a good day on the water with someone new.

Mud tires howled on the NYS Thruway for the next three hours. When we got back and were unloading the Jeep, Nikki asked when the next time we'd go fishing would be. I told her about a spot on the West Canada Creek I could take her to. I chalked the weekend up as a win.

19
Guiding

In the past three or four years, I'd gone through phases. Maybe you'd call it a cycle. I don't know what it would really be called. It doesn't matter, I suppose. Basically, I'd realize every now and then that I wasn't happy working a normal nine to five job knowing that there were people out there doing it a different way. Fishing for a living. Guiding. Or writing for a living. Or owning fly shops or building fly rods or *any* of the other *numerous things* that one could do to make a living somehow in the fly fishing and outdoors industry. Ever since I'd hung up my climbing harness and taken a normal job in a production plant, I'd been restless.

I joined the Air Force straight out of high school for no other reason than I didn't know what else to do. I didn't have any real interests besides fishing and Metallica in high school, and I'd have to say I didn't really have any useful skills. The military seemed like the thing to do, so I did it.

Not very long into it, I decided it wasn't for me; so when my four years were up, I moved on. Turning wrenches in the Air Force had turned me into a gearhead so I chased a living building hot rods and custom cars. I stayed in the Florida Panhandle where I'd been stationed but found out that working for friends wasn't such a swell idea once I figured out that I'd actually been making more money in the military. I was having fun welding on old cars and racing at the drag strip on the weekends, but it was a dead end as far as making a living went. So I moved back up home to N.Y. If I was going to struggle to live, at least I'd do it back home.

In New York I found another custom shop to work for. I was shaping metal, turning flat 18-gauge sheet metal into body panels and having a great time. But again, I found that it was a tough business. Eventually, I had enough paychecks bounce and was asked enough times if I could wait to cash my paycheck for a few days before things went south. My attitude was poor while my ambitions were high, and in the end I was fired at about the same exact moment I quit. In all truth when it came down to it, I'd quit in my head weeks earlier, they just said "you're fired" out loud first. It was the only job I was ever fired from, but at the time I remember wearing it on my sleeve with pride. I stood up for myself and said my piece, consequences be damned. Sometimes that's just how you have to handle life.

Actually, it was a couple months before the simultaneous firing and quitting that I'd first said my piece without saying a word at all. There was a big car show that we set up at each year in Syracuse, and it was simply expected that I'd be there. I was never asked, and I wasn't paid for the weekend, but I suppose that being a hot rodder it was just taken for granted that you'd want to be there and be more than happy to be. And up to that year, I always had been. But that year I'd had enough, and on Friday - a normal work day - I helped haul trailers to the show and set up our display.

The next morning, however, a Saturday - *not a normal work day* - instead of driving out to the show and spending the day talking to people about the cars we'd set up, I went fishing. I didn't call anyone and tell them. I just didn't go to the show. I was miles away on a lake catching bass and bluegills. They say a picture speaks a thousand words, but it's actions that get the bigger responses.

Up until then, since becoming a gearhead, I'd left my fishing rods and tackle boxes in closets except for maybe once or twice a year. The morning I got up and went fishing instead of going to that car show was some type of turning point for me. I remembered what it was I'd forgotten, and I started fishing on a more regular basis. I remembered what was important in life. And it wasn't all big motors and chopped tops.

I tried owning my own shop, but that collapsed on itself and almost had me in divorce court in less than a year. Things happen fast. Bad things happen even faster. I took a job in an ornamental iron works shop as a welder and fabricator, but three months in, the blacksmith had some type of mid-life crisis or something and just up and quit after, like, seventeen years. My boss asked me if I had any interest in learning to forge. Naturally, my answer was a resounding *YES*.

I found myself standing at an anvil ten hours a day creating art for the rich and famous, and on my lunches fishing the trout stream down the hill from the shop. Life was great. A job I loved with a mid-day break to try and fool trout. But when the economy crashed in 2008, it finally caught up to us in 2011. Our back logs were gone, and it was either change to fit the new economy or go away.

My boss had been at it for over thirty-five years. He'd built the business from nothing in an old barn. He'd built functional forged art for everyone from famous actors and musicians to owners of the most successful banks that were household names and people who'd owned big things; like Chrysler Building big things. He wasn't about to change the way he did things to accommodate the wealthy. He was about to retire.

So, I moved on again. I left behind a French patterned blacksmithing hammer with a handle worn perfectly to my hand, and a spot on the banks of that trout stream worn perfectly to my feet. It's the one job to this day that I know I'd have never left if things hadn't turned out the way they did. If only I'd found it years earlier.

From there I went to climbing cell towers. Why? Because everyone needs a job. I traveled all over N.Y. State and sometimes into neighboring states. Eventually, I carried more fishing gear than I did clothes and climbing gear for the week. The job was exciting, a little crazy, and the views just couldn't be beat. Life on the road was what led to me taking up fly fishing and writing. It was also the second time I found myself on the verge of divorce, but we got through it, once again.

Marriage is a series of ups and downs, after all. It's what

everyone tells you. Your parents, your relatives, friends, complete strangers...even the priest who married us. At first I almost asked him, *"How would you know?"* since he could never get married. But later, I figured he knew because he was always trying to keep couples together. He'd probably seen enough to realize that he might be better off where he was. Go figure.

The tower life took its toll over four years. It wasn't easy on our marriage, on my family life with my boys, or on my body, for that matter. I was in my mid-thirties trying to keep up with kids that were just over the drinking age. I *was* keeping up, and I was even showing some of them how it was done hundreds of feet in the air, but I couldn't keep it up forever and expect to keep my sanity. Or my marriage. I think I even came close to dying a horrible death once. And there were a couple stressful close calls. So, everyone say it with me one more time...*I quit.*

I took a job at a production plant making special alloys for the aircraft industry. Maintenance department. I hadn't ever worked what I'd referred to as a *normal job*...a job where you clocked in and clocked out, a union job where you got bounced around from day shift to night shift to working every weekend and even the holidays. I still remember the day I called it. I was walking from one building to another one afternoon with Dale Coria. We'd both started together on the same day and we'd only been there for *two weeks*. In a couple more weeks, we'd get thrown into the mix of the second and third shifts. He looked at me and saw it on my face.

"What's up, dude? You look like something's wrong." He was right, something was definitely wrong. I wasn't building a killer hot rod or pounding out a hot glowing orange leaf on the end of a length of steel. I wasn't using any of the skills I knew I had. I wasn't looking out over the world below me from three hundred feet in the air with a breeze in my face either. There was no spectacular view of rolling hills or mountains or rivers snaking through forests or distant lakes, and no fishing for a few hours after work every day. Just a dirty and noisy factory. Those days, all of them, they were behind me. Gone. I shook my head at his

question and answered without even turning to look at him that day. *"This isn't going to work. This just isn't going to work. I'll be looking for another job before the end of the year. This isn't going to work."*

Dale and I became good friends, and less than two years later when I put in my two weeks' notice, we laughed about it. We still laugh about it when we see each other. But I wasn't leaving to do anything better. I just left for another *normal job* with better hours. Monday through Friday, day shift. But I still left.

So, after four years working in production plants at what I politely call *typical and normal* jobs, I found myself divorced and miserable. What I'd always tried to avoid while working all those different jobs over all those years. Why I'd taken a *normal job*. Irony or fate? Who knew, and it didn't really matter I suppose. It just *was*. And there, once again, I started questioning why I was doing what I was doing and not doing what so many others did instead. Especially now that I had no wife.

I had friends that were guides, friends who owned fly shops. JP had a fly rod business for over twenty years now, and I'd even met someone who wrote for a living. He was traveling in a Westfall van cross country, doing book signing appearances to promote his current book while working to meet the publishing company deadline for his next!

And there I was pumping grease into the bearings of a rolling mill. I could describe what a rolling mill does, but it has nothing to do with fly fishing, so who cares? And that was my whole point...what was the point? To pay child support and die? There had to be something more. I was just too chicken to take a chance on anything else. Then the email came.

The day JP got the email from a private lodge in the Adirondacks looking for a fishing guide for a week, he decided he'd heard enough whimpering, enough talking out of my ass about my current situation. He told me it was time to put up or shut up. *"You keep saying you need to try something to make some money with the whole fly-fishing thing. This is it. You either do this and take the chance or just quit talking about any of it. Now's the time. Do it."*

I'd never used a guide, not once. I'd never guided anyone either. I didn't know what was expected of me and I never fished the lake they needed a guide on. After a couple days, I reluctantly said yes. What did I have to lose?

The idea of taking complete strangers out fly fishing on a lake I didn't know was horrifying to me at first. But by the time JP had convinced me to take the job over days of coercing, the threat-con level had been down-graded from horrifying to scary. I had him build me another 7wt, and I bought another reel and bass taper line. And in the last three days before I was supposed to take a week's vacation from work to go *"work"*, I got busy.

I sat in the house I'd just bought and tied poppers and streamers at a kitchen table that looked like a battlefield where an army of rabid chickens had gone to war with a herd of circus clown deer. It looked like the lab of a mad flyentist. I ate my breakfast on the coffee table in the living room, where I was able to find an opening among all the fly boxes and tippet spools (the fly rod tubes and various other objects of the affliction) to set down my bowl of Cap'n Crunch.

Over the month leading up to the guiding job, I went through a few stages in my head. First was the *"what the hell did I get myself into"* stage. I'd never guided or used a guide. I'm the type of guy that needs to see it done or do it myself to feel some confidence. I can't just read about it or listen to someone else talk. I was freaking myself out in my mind. I was walking into almost certain disaster the way I saw it. Certain disaster I had agreed to.

Next was the *"I need to learn everything I can about this place right now"* stage. I pummeled JP with questions daily. I'm sure he was getting tired of my constant inquiries as to the size of the lake, the depth, the clarity, the type of cover along the shore, the nature of the fish, the size of the fish, the flies he used when he'd guided there and what he thought I should tie up for my week.

It was a bass lake. Smallmouth bass. It was an average of ten or twelve feet deep, with typical weed beds, but lots of open water. A main lake and then two smaller man-made lakes along what used to be the outlet stream. And since it was summer and it was full of smallmouths, I should just pack a couple boxes of top water poppers.

I hit the final stage about a week before hand. The *"screw it, it is what it is"* stage. I had two boxes of poppers tied up by then, and they looked pretty darn good to me. I had a few damsel flies and hoppers, too, but I was banking on the poppers pulling most of the weight. *Smallmouth weren't that hard to catch*, is what I told myself, and I began to chill out about the whole thing. Maybe the hoppers would come in handy in a pinch when nothing but pan fish were biting in the heat of the day.

The only thing I had left to deal with was figuring out how I was going to deal with the clients. I had no idea who they were and could only prepare for the worst. The worst being people who'd never fly fished before. I didn't even know if I could really teach someone in such a short time frame. I've never regarded myself as much of a teacher, so that was probably my biggest fear. Having someone staring at me, waiting for answers as to why the line was ending on the water in a pile ten feet from the boat, and me not knowing what to tell them. Because I was worried about people who'd never done it and didn't know how to cast, I decided on the 7wt fly rods with heavy front taper bass lines.

I already had one 7wt that JP had built for me a couple years earlier, and it was my favorite bass rod because it loaded so much power that it shot line and wind resistant flies pretty effortlessly. So I had him build me one more. It was a duplicate of the one I already had with different color thread wraps and a slightly different handle so I could tell them apart from a distance, and I outfitted both rods with heavy front taper bass lines. The way I saw it, if any of these clients had never cast a fly rod before, the heavy front taper would give them a little more distance even on horrible casts. Anything to make them seem like they were struggling a little less had to be a good thing.

I was borrowing JP's boat, one of those modified v-bottom olive drab deals. Since my jeep had a spare tire mounted in the receiver hitch, he offered to tow the boat up for me and drop it off. JP was really going out of his way to help me out here, trying to get me out of my comfort zone and hopefully into a new one. Other than clients who'd never fly fished before that I couldn't teach, I suppose looking back my biggest fear was actually letting him down.

My mind was set at ease, mostly, when we dropped off the boat a day ahead of time. We'd gotten permission to fish the lake for a couple hours that evening so that JP could show me what he knew, and I could show up the next day with some type of a plan, not just shooting from the hip. We caught a couple bass, cruised the lake so I could get a look at the entire thing, and had a couple beers. We were just a couple buds out fishing. Suddenly the pressure was gone. It was just fishing. I'd forgotten all along that's all it was. Just fishing.

The next day, I arrived late afternoon. I was shown to my room in the lodge off the back of the kitchen, where I left my bags and met one of the two chefs who spoke with a New Zealand accent. He showed me the refrigerator where I could come in and get my lunches and dinners and seemed a very professional, but personable, guy. Then they showed me a room full of cases of soda, beer, and wine. I was to stock my cooler on the boat from this room whenever I needed to and get ice from the kitchen ice machine. I didn't even have to supply my own drinks or snacks for these people. Not a bad deal at all. The kitchen was a flurry of activity as staff and chefs prepared dinner, so I said I'd see them later and walked a dirt road to the boat launch where I'd keep JP's boat.

There was a boathouse, a massive two-story Adirondack structure on the lake right next to the main lodge, but JP's boat wasn't allowed to be stored there. The boathouse - complete with its huge waterfront deck full of Adirondack chairs, a bar, and a selection of everything from kayaks to ski boats and numerous choices in between - was only for guests. I also wasn't allowed to hang out with the guests unless specifically invited. I was hired help and therefore invisible unless needed.

I'd launch from a separate spot down the lake farther and arrive three times a day to pick up guests and take them out for a couple hours at a time, then drop them back off again before a meal. Once before breakfast, once before lunch, and then once more before dinner. Once the boat had been put in the water, the trailer had been hurried off to a hiding place. Everything at this lodge was clean and orderly, right down to the last detail. I wondered if I should have gotten a haircut. Then I decided no. It was just fishing, after all.

The down time in between clients was to be spent how I saw fit. Readying gear for the next trip, out scouting for the best spots for that time of day...I could just go fishing myself as long as I was out of sight of guests. It was even suggested that if I cared to, I could simply take a nap in my room. I laughed at the option of napping. I had a boat, fly rods, and a lake that no one - and I mean no one - was allowed to fish unless they were a guest. And they thought I might want to take a nap?

I untied the boat, pushed off, gave the motor a pull, and cruised off out across the lake to see what I could catch before the sun went down. I tied on a yellow popper striped like a bumblebee and sent out a cast over shallow water along the shore. On the third pop, it disappeared in a splash. The line went tight. Across the lake laughter and happy voices carried from the party going on out on the boathouse deck. Some of the voices would be in my boat at 6am the next day. How could this go badly? It was only fishing.

*****

This lake was so dark, it was like looking into a 2-liter bottle of Coca-Cola. On some waters you can move along the shoreline, searching. Your baseball hat and a raised hand shielding eyes from a sun just barely beginning to break the tree line, its first blinding rays piercing through the tops of the trees where they meet the sky like ragged spear points against pale blue. On some lakes you could do that and spot fish...see them, cast to them. But not on this lake. On this lake, there was no sight fishing. The smallmouth bass themselves were so dark. And with the island on the lake with the ospreys that circled looking for a meal, they stayed down well below the surface, camouflaged to the point of invisibility. Their bronze was more of a patina, like a brass hinge that had seen a hundred years and never a polish rag. The water was the color of Coca-Cola. The bass were the same. You cast to a likely spot and hoped for the best.

The places we find ourselves at in life aren't only just physical places. The places I'm referring to are mental. But in many instances, it's a physical place that changes where we are mentally. I won't hide the fact anymore that I was struggling with depression quite a bit. I'm not sure if I had been ashamed, or embarrassed, or if it's just my nature to ignore the obvious and hide it with a smile when it's something that creates discomfort, unrest, or an all-out desire to withdraw from everything and everyone. I've often smiled to those around me when things were bad just so I wouldn't have to talk about it.

The fish that swim in the rivers and lakes were then - and are still now - often the only thing I can find myself relating to on most days. We were just trying to survive each day, to stay cool and calm in a world ready to eat us at the first sign of weakness. Neither of us really wanted to be found, yet here I was, out on a remote lake with complete strangers, trying to find them.

I guided a handful of complete strangers over a period of four days. Out of about a dozen guests that I took out to fish, only two had ever cast a fly rod before. Every trip out was more or less the same, but always different. First there was getting to know each other; the part where they'd tell me that they had never fly fished but had always thought it was just for trout, or that they'd never even really fished at all. One woman admitted to using the cliché child's Snoopy fishing pole once while at a camp with someone else's kids, and that was the whole extent of her fishing experience.

Next there was the *"This is the principle of why a fly rod works"* speech and demonstration. I quickly explained to them as simply as possible that the line was the weight, the only reason the weightless fly could be cast, that the rod was what propelled the line, and in the end, *it's only fishing.* You had to forget that you'd never done it before and just cast. Ten and two, flicking paint off of a brush, blah, blah, blah. I'd tell them pretty loops were fun and nice to look at, but that they were smallmouth bass we were chasing. And smallmouth bass care less about how the line does or doesn't gently fall to the water and more about whether they can eat something they see moving.

If they could just get the popper out away from the boat fifteen feet or so, they'd have a good chance at seeing a splash, and probably even a fish. I only had these people for a couple hours most of the time, three and a half or so at best. I wanted to spend ninety-eight percent of the time fishing, and only two percent of it being them worrying about not knowing how to do it. The goal was fun and forgetting everything else not on the lake; otherwise, what's the point?

Next came the awkward casting and the banter that accompanied it. *"Oh, that was a bad one." "Oh, that's not what I wanted to do at all." "Whoops, I'm tangled. I don't know how I did that."* This went on for a little bit, but a wonderful thing happened each time out during this phase of the trips. They'd be struggling with trying to figure out the whole casting thing, when the last thing they expected would happen. Their popper would disappear in a splash - sometimes nothing more than a small boil, other times a violent attack. They were never ready for it and would freeze up at the sight and sound of me yelling, *"Set it! Set the hook!"* They'd always miss the first one.

And then, just like that, the nervous banter during the clumsy casting would come to an end, replaced by focus; a new determination fueled by proof that it was possible, and a great deal of new hope. The boat would become all but completely silent after the initial excitement. There were only new fly anglers trying to catch a fish, and a guide at the oars keeping them within reach of the most likely water.

It was one of the greatest things I've ever been a part of. The conversations would eventually begin again, but now instead of random dialogs about what family or friends had been up to or who had been doing what at work, they turned to questions about this whole fly-fishing thing that was now enveloping their mind. What were they doing wrong in their cast? They wanted me to watch and tell them. What did they do when they hooked a fish? What kind of flies would they use for other fish? Would they use these same rods? Smaller? Bigger? Where was my favorite place to fly fish? My biggest fish? How long had I been fly fishing? Could they do it where they came from…California? Texas? Oklahoma? Long Island? The answer was you can fly fish for practically anything, anywhere. The gears were turning in their heads, I could see it.

There was a cooler on the boat, and while it was my seat while at the oars, it also contained a good mix of water, beer, wine, and other such celebratory beverages. But most of the time, no one wanted to stop for a drink. They wanted to keep casting after that first miss. It was great. I was enjoying it immensely.

After the loss of a yellow popper with black bumblebee stripes to a tree branch, I was retrieving a new one from my neatly arranged popper box and the client who'd lost the popper remarked at how professional the box looked. He asked if I'd tied everything in it. I said I had, but that it was too early in the week to be judging books by covers, or guides by fly boxes. I told him that I tried to live my life the same way I organized my fly boxes…with good intentions; but just like the fly boxes, good intentions are only so good and last only so long, and that sooner or later you go to the box to find a specific fly that will change your luck for the better and find only an unorganized mess. Chaos was probably the better word. Just ask my ex-wife.

Most everyone over the four days caught a fish, if not a

couple, and they were all thrilled having never fly fished before and each only having an honest couple hours' time at it. After they'd held their first fish in their hands, I'd be sure to tell them the true story of my first fish on a fly rod, a four-inch creek chub on a dry fly that took me the better part of six months to finally catch. I was hell bent on learning it all on my own and suffered through it the whole time, wondering if it was all worth it for months of casting to end with a minnow. Obviously, I'd tell them, *it was*. Because here I was, years later, on the lake with them.

There were a handful of great stories that came out of that week. The reason for the week at this remote and extremely private lodge was a birthday. Stacey was the birthday girl, and she'd brought along about thirty friends and family members, including her son Ethan who was about fourteen, from what I could tell. He was a well-mannered young man, and we bonded almost immediately. They both fished, but not nearly often enough, as they put it, since Stacey seemed to be in the upper echelons of the corporate legal world. Like many people in her position, I could only imagine that *getting away from it all* was a challenge to say the least.

They were my first clients on the first morning. The first trip out was a bust. Some casting instruction, a couple missed fish, but nothing hooked or landed. But the quiet and stillness of an Adirondack lake at six o'clock on a summer morning is something to behold all on its own, fish or not. As we motored away from the boathouse deck, the sky was the beginning of a dull blue, nothing more. The lake out in front of us was a cloud, gray and billowing, visibility was at about thirty feet. But there was nothing ominous about it. Nothing frightening or alarming. There was simply peace.

I sat on the Yeti cooler in the middle of the boat and rowed along the lake shore to our right while Ethan stood on the bow and Stacey stood on the rear bench platform in front of the motor. Besides the occasional red squirrel that would chatter at us from shore, in the beginning when the fog was at its thickest and the sky at its dullest, there was hardly any sound except for the oars squeaking in the gunnels and the foam poppers punching through the air. Watching fog go through its changes has always fascinated me, and while Ethan and Stacey were concentrating on making their first awkward casts, I would see them pause and look out at the fog now and then, too. It was the stuff you wish everyone could see - really stop and take notice - but most get too busy to take in their surroundings during their normal daily grinds.

First, the fog was a cloud and we were in it. The cloud doesn't move, it's just gray, dull, and wet; it's just there, everywhere. But as it changes, the fog goes through stages. The next stage is the cloud begins to move. It's still tall, still blocks out everything, but voids begin to emerge, the cloud dancing on end around them like tall billowing mountains slowly spinning and tearing off one another. It's like some kind of fantasy wonderland out of an old fairytale.

Next, it goes from a fairytale to a horror movie as the cloud's top side begins to burn off and it's left as a few feet tall. It churns, no longer billowy, but instead tearing and moving itself as if it's alive and moving in all directions at once. Like it's covering water, searching.

Finally, now hovering on the surface of the water and only an inch or so of wisps, it's almost like a moving *film* on the water. Something alive but fading fast.

At some point between the horror movie phase and the fading wisps, the sky had become bright, the sun showing through the trees as it crested the ridge behind the lodge. And along with the light came all the noise. There must've been a thousand blue jays in the forest surrounding the lake, and hundreds of other birds and the chattering red squirrels. It went from dead silent to the exact and extreme opposite in a matter of a moment. The screeches of the blue jays and the chattering squirrels made it sound like a jungle straight out of the old black and white Tarzan movies I'd watched as a child on my grandmother's black and white TV. They'd always been one of my favorites, and now I felt as if I was in one. Thankfully, there were no arrows bouncing off the boat.

Ethan and Stacey made cast after cast, concentrating on the prize they hoped to earn. But it wasn't to be on their first time out. They did miss a couple hook sets, the way most anyone would who's never fished a popper with a fly rod for bass before usually does. The poppers disappeared in a slurp each time, but neither was ready for it. I imagine they were probably thinking in their heads that this fly-fishing thing wasn't going to work, or that I didn't know where the fish were, or they were contemplating the casting in their heads after the popper had touched down. Either way, they weren't ready for the strikes. When they'd finally realized the fly was gone, it was too late to set a hook. The popper simply resurfaced.

It's something all new fly anglers do, but I told them not to feel bad, I still did it. I'll make a good cast, then look down at my feet to see if I'm stepping on fly line or maybe it's caught underneath the end of the push poll. That's when a bass makes the grab, and I look up and realize all too late my missed opportunity. That's usually when JP gives me that astonished look, the one that says *I can't believe you did it AGAIN*. I told them in a way that meant they were all caught up to me and my bass fishing skills in about two hours, to what had taken me years. But they were happy and smiling when I pulled up alongside the boathouse deck and they hopped out. They both agreed that every day should start as this one had. I thought in my head, *if only they could*.

A sign-up sheet was placed in the dining hall. Guests would grab slots and the sheet would be placed in my room at the end of each night. I knew I must've been doing something right, because after the first day the sheet for the second was full of names, most of which were repeats. And they were written in, then crossed out, and then moved to other time slots with different names. It looked as though everyone was excited to go out and fish, and that they were looking to all fish with each other eventually through the week. They were jockeying for the best times and trying to get everyone who wanted to go out on the boat paired up with old friends and family they hadn't seen in a while. The way anyone would want it, really.

The way I saw it, if the guests weren't happy about their trips out onto the lake, I'd most likely find an empty sheet. It was quite the opposite. I was actually getting requests for additional slots. The lodge manager wanted to be sure that I was going to be ok with going out more often than we originally agreed on, and I assured him I was more than fine with it. If I was there, I wanted to be on the water. And if I was on the water, I thought it was spectacular that these people wanted to be out there too, considering they'd never touched a fly rod before. I didn't need to rest during the day. I was there for them.

Mark and Tom were brothers. Mark lived in LA, and Tom Oklahoma. They both fished, but neither had ever done it on the fly. It was the recipe for my two favorite guests to take out over the week. They went out with me more than once, and so we got to know each other fairly well; as well as you can get to know someone you've only just met and fished with on a fourteen-foot boat on a quiet Adirondack lake, anyway. Which, as you might guess, is pretty well in the end. The fact that they were brothers who didn't live close to each other was what made the time on the lake with them my favorite. I have two brothers myself that I hardly ever see, so I know how much fun - and how important it is - for brothers to reconnect. Brothers need to tell stories about the old days; they need to fill each other in on what's been going on, and they can get a little competitive.

Out of the entire guest list, they were both probably the best casters, other than Ethan who seemed like a natural. They didn't have the tightest loops and might have rocked the boat a little now and then, putting a little too much body into their casts, but all in all, they showed the most improvement the quickest. And they caught a lot of fish.

One of the afternoons I had them casting into a dark and sheltered cove on the back third lake. They were working a half sunken tree trunk that formed the edge of the water about the way a curb forms the edge of a street. I knew the cove was going to have a lot of fish in it, it was just too good not to. The sun was high, but it was still sheltered and somewhat shaded. Up to this point, neither of the brothers had caught a fish yet. They'd been fishing for about a half hour without so much as a strike, so in their heads they were probably thinking the day would be a bust, but they were humoring me.

Mark was telling us a story of how he and his wife had just bought a new house and before they'd left, they hired a new gardener. The story went that he'd noticed the gardener working around his neighbor's house and so he introduced himself. He told the man that he'd just moved in and was looking for a lawn man. He knew he'd misspoken by the ice cold look on his face, but it was too late. The man quipped up and corrected Mark, "*I'm a gardener, NOT a lawn man.*" After an awkward apology and some more awkward small talk, he ended up hiring the man.

Tom and I both laughed, and Tom told him he'd be lucky when they got back home to find all the bushes and flowers still planted in their places. We all laughed with scenes in our heads of uprooted plants and shrubs chopped off at the ground piled on his front porch with a snooty note on the door that read *Lawn Man Indeed!*

Just as we were finishing our laughs, Tom began to say something, but then Mark's popper was lost in a splash alongside that half sunken tree trunk. Mark had that look on his face that said he was wondering if we saw it at the same time I was yelling "*Set the hook!*" But he missed it. The popper floated back to the top. Suddenly, seeing that this fly-fishing thing could actually work, and I imagine one brother seeing the other brother *almost* catch the first fish, the conversation went silent. Eyes were affixed on targets; the casting became focused and serious. The game was on.

Sitting on the cooler, I'd pivot the boat with the oars and move it up and down the shoreline, telling them both where I thought they should cast. I don't remember which one caught the first fish, because frankly at that moment, it didn't really matter. All that mattered was they had both just become believers. For the next two hours, I moved them up and down the shore of that back lake. We'd hit a stretch of shoreline where they'd both be landing little smallmouths one after the other, and when they'd been pressured enough to quit biting, I'd fire up the motor and move to another shore. The two brothers, it seemed in my mind, were suddenly about twenty years younger.

Tom caught the biggest fish of the day out of all the guests, and I think he had the biggest smile out of everyone that day, too. He was standing on the bow and made a cast that landed absolutely perfectly next to a small lily pad patch about the size of a kitchen table. When the 7wt doubled over, I didn't have to tell him to set it; the hook was already firmly in place. I got a great photo of him holding up a nice three-pound smallmouth. If it wasn't for the heat of the day, I think they'd almost have skipped happy hour.

Artemis was a lawyer. She did mostly pro bono work, tough cases involving kids. She'd never fished before other than out on a deep-sea charter once, and she stated more than once - in a joking manner but still serious from what I could tell - that she didn't believe a little piece of foam with a couple feathers could catch a fish. Her partner for their slot was Ellen. Ellen was a pharmacist. She'd never fished a day in her life.

Neither one of them really got the casting down, but they tried. I also don't believe that either one of them cared if they caught a fish or not, which was why I *really* wanted one of them to catch one. I don't think either one of them thought they would. They were just out to enjoy some time on the lake and catch up.

Drifting on a light breeze, I had them fishing to a weedy shoreline. Neither one could get their cast out more than about fifteen feet, so I was using the wind to our advantage instead of the noisy oar locks and keeping them about sixteen or seventeen feet off the weed line, which seemed to keep most of their casts within a foot of the weeds, give or take. Artemis was simply lifting her line off the water, making a single back cast, and plopping her foam frog popper back down in one single forward cast. It was efficient, so I told her if it worked, go with it. She wasn't getting it any farther with two or ten more back casts anyhow, so it indeed was efficient casting.

Ellen was the exact opposite. She made her forward and back casts twice as fast as the line's actual speed, and so she'd end up flailing like a fourteen-year-old marching with the school band with one of those sticks with the ribbon on the end of it; only her body language said that at the end of that ribbon was a ten-pound lead weight. It was awkward and couldn't be corrected in the time we had. So I just flipped up my shirt collar, pulled down my hat tight, and kept low on the cooler. Neither one thought they had a chance in hell of catching a fish. Until Ellen missed her first one.

We were alongside a weed bed to our right, and honestly were only about ten feet off it. She hurled line and popper overhead, the line slashed through the air with the rod making the sound of multiple fighter jets passing by. I kept my head down but watched the water. Her popper landed in the most perfect spot; I *knew* there was a strike coming. The weed bed had a small cut-in, an opening about the size of the end of the oar, and the popper landed at the back edge of it, just barley touching the weeds. I said out loud, *"Oh, that's a fish if I ever saw one. Get ready."* She asked me what I meant but before I could tell her to get ready for a fish, *splash*, the popper was gone. She pulled up on the rod to set the hook on a twenty-foot great white. The popper sailed through the air overhead and landed on the other side of the boat.

Now both women were suddenly intent on catching a fish. Artemis couldn't believe that she'd just seen a fish almost caught with a piece of foam; she must have said it laughing in disbelief three times. Ellen made another landing practically on the weeds, and another splash. This time she set the hook easier but took too long and missed another one. She missed a third. The women were whooping it up; they couldn't get over how close they were coming to catching something, and apparently it wasn't a fluke, since between the two of them they'd missed four so far.

On the fifth one, Ellen set the hook, but let go of all the slack line in her other hand. And so, for a quick hook-setting second, the line was tight and then in the blink of an eye went completely slack. I knew the fish was still on as I followed the line down into the dark under the weeds with my eyes, but if she didn't pick up the slack fast it would probably be off and another one gone.

I dove backwards towards the side of the boat and at her feet, reached out with both arms, grabbed the line, and yanked up, hand lining it in faster than a fat guy sucking in a long piece of spaghetti. I jumped up and held a twelve-inch smallmouth bass in front of her and I couldn't help but yell *YES!* The two women suddenly sounded like a football stadium filled to capacity.

As I stood next to Ellen holding the fish in front of her so Artemis could take a picture, I suddenly felt it. *I felt like a guide.*

On one of the days as I was dropping off a couple guests back at the boathouse, a young woman came out to the boat and asked if I was taking anyone else out soon and I told her not for a couple hours. She asked if I would be able to take her and her son out for a short ride. Her son was young, and she didn't know how long he would last or if I'd even take them out with him only being about four. Naturally, I told her to grab him a life jacket and we'd be off.

Jessica wanted to give the fly rod a shot but was really just looking to take her son Etienne out on the boat for a ride. Who was I to object? She gave it a shot while he played with the net pretending to catch fish off the side, and after a few casts decided she was happy just sitting and watching. I felt funny being the one to fish, so when she asked if I might try to show Etienne how to do it, I thought it was worth a shot. The 7wt was huge for him, and he really didn't care about the casting part, but he really wanted to make the popper splash. So I came up with a plan.

I told him that he was going to tell me where to cast. Then I'd cast it to the spot he wanted it, and while I held the rod, he'd strip the line and work the popper. So, he pointed to the left side of a lily pad patch, and I sent the line and popper overhead and into the general area he pointed out; then I told him to take the line in his hand and give it a good jerk. The popper made a *"gloop"* sound and water showered out in front of it. He went to jerk it again and I told him to wait, count to five, and then do it. He counted slowly to five and gave it another good tug. I told him to keep counting to five in between each tug, and he did. But each time, he sped up his counting.

Little boys are impatient. I can remember being on ponds with my grandfather as a very young boy. We'd cast out worms suspended under bobbers, and he would let his sit for what seemed like hours without ever touching his fishing pole. I, on the other hand, would reel mine in every two minutes to check the worm and cast to somewhere different and better. Little boys like action. *They are not patient.* Etienne was speeding up his counting faster between each pop now.

1…2…3…4…5, POP! 1…2…3…4…5, POP! 1…2…3…4…5, POP! Before I knew it he, was standing at my side pulling in the fly line hand over hand with a grin from ear to ear, the popper leaving a wake like a speedboat at full throttle throwing a rooster tail in a no wake zone. Loud and obnoxious. And then a bass smashed it! Etienne felt the line pull back through his hands and shot a puzzled but excited look up at me and I hollered, *"Get the net!"*

He spun around two times in his excitement and then grabbed up the net that was easily two feet longer than he was tall and sunk it in the water next to the boat. He watched the bass fight at the side of the boat the way a cat would look down into a fish bowl getting ready to swat, and as he made frantically slow scoops that came nowhere near the fish, I finally was able to steer it into the net and he yelled. It was one of those little kid yells that sounds like an adult at a sporting event yelling like a little kid. He had all he could do to lift it out of the water. I honestly don't know who was smiling bigger, Etienne, Jessica, or me. I told him it was his fish, he'd caught it, and we took a couple pictures. They were telling the story back at the boathouse before I was even pulling away.

There were so many stories, so many great moments. Too many to keep going on about. Like the huge buck we saw crossing the stream in front of us between the first and second lakes. It was easily over two-hundred pounds and had a summer rack in velvet that was on its way to being truly impressive by the time fall came around. It stood in the stream rather stoically, the water just covering the bottom of its muscular chest and turned and walked out of the stream and disappeared into the woods to our left as if it had rehearsed its exit a thousand times in preparation for that days performance.

Or how Stacey's father literally gave me the shirt off his back. While out on the lake, we were talking and getting to know each other - the way it happens when you're fishing - and I discovered that he was from Modesto, California. He was wearing a t-shirt from a big car show out there. I told him I knew about Modesto because of the car show on his shirt. I'd not only built hot rods in a past life, but I'd built a 1955 Chevy because of the one Bob Falfa drove in the movie "American Graffiti." He asked if I'd ever been to Modesto for the show, but I told him no. I would've loved to when I was into the car scene, but it was one I never got to see.

On the final day, as I was dropping off the last guests after the very last trip out, I found Lou waiting for me on the boat house dock. In his hand was the t-shirt he'd been wearing when I'd taken him out. I didn't know what to say. I said thank you, of course, but it seemed a little generic for such a gesture. But on the morning of the final day, Stacey and her father came back out with me one last time. She'd yet to catch a fish. It was now or never. I'm not saying I was feeling any pressure, but I sure wanted her to hook into one and get it in her hands.

She was standing on the back of the boat by the motor, casting from the rear bench platform, when her popper vanished in a huge and loud boil only ten feet from the boat. She lifted the rod and set the hook, and that's when the smallmouth put the transmission in granny low. It pulled straight down to the bottom and stayed there. Stacey looked at me with huge round eyes and the rod doubled over as the line began to head away from the boat, and then when it couldn't go any farther, it would change directions and put all its energy into its new course. Twice, she got it up close enough to the surface to make out the golden flashes of its belly, and it must have done this before because it was an expert at dodging my net. It was impressive, really. And a little embarrassing.

It must've found some new motivation to escape because I could see the fear in Stacey's eyes as the rod began to vibrate while her knuckles went white. "What do I *do*!? Should I *pull*!?" Before I could answer, she hunched over the fly rod handle, two-handing it and looking like a football player protecting the ball in his hands from an onslaught of opposition. She gave it all she had to yank the fish from the Coca-Cola colored water below. My mind panicked; I figured the leader was going to break for sure, and then it happened. The fish decided if she wanted it to come up, well then by God it was coming up.

The rod was loaded with all kinds of bend, the leader stretched to its limit, and the bass propelled itself upward. The rod shot the fish like a catapult, the bass decided if it was going to go out, it was going out in style, and as it passed over Stacey's head, I reached out beside the boat with my long net and caught it at about shoulder level...three feet out over the water. Her father was in the front of the boat and I believe I heard her stop breathing for a second over his explosion of laughter. We high-fived. Dropping them off at the boathouse for breakfast, I was reliving the whole thing over in my head and trying to decide if I felt like a fishing guide or someone who'd just been fishing with a couple friends. I decided both.

20

Bass

I've been told – more than once - that teaching your wife or girlfriend is best left to someone else. The task can be one of imminent strife, one that may be an innocent enough attempt to draw another into what it is that you love so much but ends in shouting, crying, and sleeping on the couch. To be clear, I found myself enjoying sleeping on a couch eventually. So that didn't even make me flinch. I'd been doing it for the better part of a year when I finally bought my own house. I didn't have a bed when it came time to move in. I didn't even look for one. To this day, my bed is the living room couch. I'm perfectly happy with the arrangement.

Not having a bed makes things simpler. I have a couple blankets, but no bed set that needs to be washed. All the same, no bed that needs to be made. I don't even have a bedroom. What most would use for their bedroom, I use as a laundry room. I set up a bedroom for the boys when they stay at my house, but the living room does just fine for me. I really don't see the need for a bed or bedroom at this point.

Of course, I don't see the need to mow the lawn either, something the neighbors had subtly hinted at over the first year in various ways. First, about a month after moving in, the guy across the street struck up a conversation with me. It ended with him giving me a push mower. It was an "extra" he had in the shed and he thought maybe I'd want it. Subtle.

Then halfway through the summer, the neighbor on my right mowed my side lawn, the one butting up to his. Of course, that was after a quick conversation as I was loading up the Jeep to take the boys fishing for the weekend for the third time of the summer. He'd said something about wishing he had more time to do the same with his kids, but the yard work was too much to break away from at the moment. I, of course, responded - as I put the shift lever in reverse - that everyone has their own priorities. He scowled. I looked at Jake and Carter and proclaimed, "And we're off!"

The following week, I was inside tying flies after work one day and I heard a mower closer to my house than normal. I looked out to see him mowing my lawn on his side. In his defense, mine was easily several inches taller than his and the contrast looked pretty horrible, if you payed attention to such things. I almost went out and told him he didn't need to, but then I thought about it. If he was willing to take care of that side this time, it was giving me more time to finish tying flies for the coming weekend chasing brook trout. And if I only had half as much to mow the next day, then I might even have a little time to fish before I fired up the mower. And a little more time to give Nikki casting lessons on the creek. What are neighbors for?

But back to teaching a girlfriend to fly fish. There are stories of success, but it's pretty much common knowledge that you don't attempt it. Things can get ugly fast. But Nicole really wanted to learn. So on the days that I didn't have Jake and Carter out there with me, I was finding myself waiting for her to get out of work. We'd put on shorts and water shoes and I'd hand her a 5wt. It only takes about a minute to walk to the creek from my back door, maybe two and a half once the weeds have grown in as tall as our fly rods and hidden all the downed trees.

She was doing ok with the shorter casts but would struggle with the longer ones. But no one was worried. That's to be expected, because that's just about how most people start out. But on the creek it didn't matter because the creek didn't call for many long casts. A simple short twenty-footer can put you on a smallmouth easily. And they're smallmouths, so it doesn't have to be a tight and quiet cast either. She didn't catch many fish at first, but she seemed both determined to not quit, and happy to just be out there. Which is really all anyone can ever ask for without sounding ungrateful. In my mind, anyhow.

You've got to be content in not catching anything before you can settle in to becoming a decent fly angler. Fly fishing is inherently peaceful. It's why we do it opposed to whipping hard plastic lures with huge treble hooks clanging all over the place. If you're going to go fly fishing and you're just getting mad and frustrated the whole time, you've missed the whole point, negated the entire reason for going in the first place. But you've definitely got to be able to handle getting skunked now and then.

The way I see it, we think we're in control of everything these days with all the technology at our fingers. We can order pizzas, buy tickets, pay bills, and even turn on the lights at home from the other side of the country if we so please by a few taps and swipes. We can make everything we want to happen, *happen right now*. But a day fishing, that'll set you straight.

Sure, we have great days where we catch a lot or catch the big ones. But there are always those days that put you in your place and remind you that you can't control it all. To see her out there concentrating on learning to cast, coming up fishless, but still taking the time to smell the roses was a relief.

I won't fish with someone who gets mad at losing fish or getting skunked. We all use four-letter words when we lose one, but I do it the same way I'd heckle a good friend for being better at something or proving me wrong. If I'm out with someone for the first time and they're genuinely angry that they didn't land one or haven't caught enough, that's probably the first and last time we fish together. Life's too short to be angry at what you claim to love. They're only fish, after all. It really can't be anyone's fault but your own. She was more than happy to be with me on the water. The rest was icing on the cake.

After a while, though, I knew it was starting to aggravate her a little that I'd cast to places that she'd made casts to and catch fish that she didn't. Who wouldn't? I didn't mean to, I'm not a dick. But I'd figure after she'd made several casts to a spot that there was nothing there. And when she'd ask me what she was doing wrong I'd show her how I would approach the same spot, how'd I'd make my cast, and then there'd be a splash and I'd get the *you're an asshole* look from her. And then I'd feel like one, naturally.

I kind of enjoy doing that sort of thing around JP and our other buddy John Montefusco; it gets some good laughs. The same way you get laughs out of someone wiping out on a bicycle of tripping over nothing and dropping a birthday cake on someone's lap. No, not everyone thinks it's funny, but it gets laughs all the same. But done to her, it lost its comic value.

So, I decided to take her to a couple different places where I was fairly sure she'd catch something. Plus, I figured she was ready for a change of scenery. The creek was nice, but it was in town. Cars passed all the time and there was the inevitable trash you'd come across. So I took her an hour north into the Adirondacks to my favorite brook trout stream. I always felt like I couldn't lose when I went there. And really it was so beautiful, you couldn't.

I strung up a short 3wt, the first Beaver Meadow JP had ever built for me and tied on a small streamer no more than an inch long. Below some small waterfalls, she made a few casts and finally one ended with a good bend in the rod. Smallmouth bass are known to be great fighters, and even a twelve-inch smallie can put up a nice fight. Now put that twelve-inch smallie on a 3wt fly rod, and you've got a party.

She was casting across the current maybe fifteen feet and stripping the streamer over an underwater rock garden of huge boulders. They formed countless black holes in the depths where they rested against each other, perfect ambush opportunities. When you spot it, you just know there's got to be a fish in every dark crevice you can pick out. Whether there actually is or not doesn't matter in a spot like that; you'll make fifty casts to it never catching anything. But you know for certain in your mind that they have to be there. Thankfully, on that day, they were.

Nikki smiled from ear to ear like an eight-year-old kid who'd gotten the pony they'd asked for on Christmas morning. I most likely did, too. It was ironic, in a cool way, when I thought about it later. It was really the first fish she caught on the fly, and I'd christened that fly rod with its first fish in the same place years before. I took a couple pictures of her holding the little tiger striped bass and then she released it. I made a couple casts of my own, came up with nothing but a couple missed strikes, and we moved up stream.

I knew the spot well and it wasn't very long before she caught her first brook trout. She ended up with two fish in a short time, a bass and a brookie, and the walk in had taken longer than the time to catch them both. The way it should always be. The short road trip had been a success.

A couple weeks later, I loaded the canoe on the Jeep and gathered my 7wts and a couple fly boxes full of poppers, and we drove south to Cobleskill. The family farm couldn't be a strike-out when it came to largemouth bass and sunfish; it seemed impossible to even consider such a scenario. I'm sure in my forty-three years on this planet that there must've been at least one trip there when I'd gotten skunked, but I can't recall one. Slow days, yes. Completely fishless days? I search my memories hard and come up with nothing.

The lake has a name I never speak. I only discovered it had a name some fifteen years ago while looking for it on Google Earth, and I'll admit that after growing up only calling it the "farm lake" and then finding out later in life that it actually had a name was slightly disappointing. It was like we suddenly weren't the only ones to ever know about it. But finding out it had a name wasn't a complete surprise. I knew it had a history.

When I was young, my grandfather had told me that the small lake was actually a reservoir built back in the days of steam engines for the purpose of supplying water to the train tracks downhill below the lake. My father mentioned once that when he'd fished it as a boy; they caught rainbow trout. I asked my grandfather about that and he told me it wasn't a lie, that at some point the lake had been part of a fish and game club and they stocked it with trout. Quite a few years later, I found out that my great-grandfather had actually fly fished there. And I thought that was pretty cool since it was around the same time I was learning to fly fish myself.

Eventually, the fish and game club quit stocking the lake with trout and the bass and sunfish took over completely. I can only imagine that the club decided the cost of the stocking wasn't worth it since they couldn't have survived very well in it. It does have one deep area where it gets a little over twenty feet, but for the most part, it's a very warm water lake, full of lily pad patches and weed beds. The quintessential farm pond full of largemouth bass and pan fish.

I'd always fought with whether to call it a big pond or a small lake, but once I found it labeled as a named lake on the map, I never really called it a pond again. Ten or twelve acres in the middle of two or three different farms is what I refer to as the water I grew up on, even if it was only on four or five weekends a summer. Outside of family, I'd only ever taken JP and his wife, Bobbi Jo, and my good friend Chris who'd let me live in his basement for half a year, to the farm lake. Basically, if Nikki didn't like it, I'd probably end the relationship. But she loved it. As if it were even possible for anyone not to love it.

In the spring, the cows were *sold down the road*. This is how it was put to me as we sat in the kitchen of the old farmhouse on a humid and sunny Saturday morning. I'd sat in this kitchen, in these same chairs, at this same table, watching hummingbirds through the same window hover around those same birdfeeders for the past...well, I never really knew how many years it had been.

I'm forty-three now, and my grandfather probably started bringing me here to fish the lake when I was six or seven, but it could've been closer to eight. I'm old enough now to say things like I've been visiting the farm for a long time now, or for a good many years, or since I was a little kid. There are a great many people I could even tell "*I've been fishing there longer than you've been alive."* You know, stuff that only someone as old as me or older can say, but we can say it with some kind of pride, because we've made it this far.

It was an odd feeling seeing the barn unused, the weeds growing up in front of the milk house door that I'd always walked through to report on the fishing at the end of the day before saying goodbye and driving back home. I wondered what becomes of barn cats that are used to drinking from milk pans during the milking hours when cows get sold down the road. Memories flooded my mind as I navigated the Jeep around the barn on what had last year been a beaten down dirt tractor path, but this year overgrown with weeds and saplings reaching in the windows as the winch bumper pushed over thistle bushes.

Looking through the windshield, I saw myself, much younger - about twelve - standing on the back side of the barnyard, playing with the farm dog, a black and white border collie. I was throwing a butternut into the corn field, and the dog would tear off at lightning speed after it. I was amazed and delighted every time that she could track down that butternut and bring it back, excited for me to throw it again.

Driving through several pastures on the way to the lake, the gates were always a challenge, each one different. All were three strands of barbed wire with two or three uprights, but they were all securely closed by a similar but different means. One gate had an old piece of electrical wire, most likely orange that had faded to almost white that you had to fight to pull over a fence post. Another had old bungee straps, the old black rubber ones with the "S" hooks that you had to wind around the right amount of times and hook back to themselves. The final one before the lake pasture was secured closed with bailing twine. Only it was a long piece that had broken and been knotted back together over and over again so that it was difficult and took some studying before you could find the actual end of it.

I couldn't remember the first time I'd walked ahead of my grandfather's truck to open the gates and close them behind us, but I remembered as I got older being proud to do it. Opening and closing the gates was a rite of passage to me. When I was a little kid, I'd watched from the truck's cab as my grandfather got out and wrestled with each one. Once I was big enough and strong enough to work the gates, it was like I'd become an adult. In my young mind, being trusted enough to keep the cows where they belonged and taking the place of my grandfather at the gates, I was a man.

It's really something to look back on a grandfather getting older and letting you do the work because you are, too. It's something else years later - the same but different - to realize now what you didn't realize then. It meant you were both getting older and that all things pass with time, including us.

This trip, this was the first time I could drive across the entire farm from the house to the lake, and not have to stop to open or close a single gate. You'd think it would make the drive in faster, but somehow it made it seem longer. Where I'd normally stop to open a gate and look back on a time before when maybe the bull had charged or the cows had all crowded around as if to inspect me, now I drove through open gates pushing through grass and saplings and thistle bushes taller than the hood of the Jeep, thinking that this could be the last summer I ever got to. It had always been a possibility, but now it seemed a harsh reality. All farms get sold sooner or later. It was ironic, the fields were so full of tall grass and thistle bushes and saplings. But they seemed so empty.

We climbed the last steep hill up to the lake lot, passed through the final open gate, and as branches from overhanging trees clawed at the canoe on the roof, I looked back to a time where the lake was visible from this point. Years and years ago. The lake was no longer visible until the Jeep would clear the other end of this tunnel of old growth trees above and the new growth trees on the fence line on our right. The trees on the right had begun to grow several years ago when the lake lot had gotten too far away from the barn and house to bother to use anymore. Gone long ago were the days of fishing while cows chewed their cud twenty feet behind you in the shade of the willows.

Clearing the tunnel of foliage, I stopped so Nikki could take in the view of the lake down below the same way I would every trip. I remembered a time when foreign soil in a hostel land was under my boots and closing my eyes at night I'd see this view and know that someday soon I'd be back to that very spot feeling the breeze as the willow trees down along the lake swayed in sunlight. Their backdrop the shimmering water just beyond them.

I couldn't shake those thoughts of the farm becoming nothing more than a memory to me, but when we finally arrived at the water's edge, I shifted gears the best I could. I put the canoe in the water and rigged up two 7wts with foam poppers. Dragonflies hovered and dive bombed the surface everywhere, hundreds of them. Dragonflies, damsel flies, browns, blacks, blues, oranges, greens. And where they hovered too long, fish were death from below. Out on the lake, twenty or thirty swallows performed acrobatic feats like skilled dog fighters as they swooped down and splashed and lifted and barrel rolled. I could only assume feasting the same as the fish. The lake was alive, the sky a cloudless and bright blue, the heat climbing. It was the perfect day to be here. The stars had aligned.

While I was stringing up the two 7wts, Nikki was asking questions. *"Do you want to set up the chairs and get stuff ready for lunch? Get the fire ready? Do you want to get this out of the Jeep? Do you want to get that out of the Jeep?"* For every question she asked, two fish could be heard clobbering a dragon or damsel fly in the background. It was one of those mornings where you didn't have to see the fish jumping, *you could hear them.*

I was trying to concentrate on pulling a bass taper fly line through the guides of the second rod when she asked another question about what I wanted to do. I tried not to be short with her, but I answered her with a mere eight words; *"I just want to get on the water. The longer we stand here on dry land, the more fish we're missing,"* and kept threading line through guides. She laughed and said, "*Ok, fair enough*", as another splash was heard close to the shore on the other side of some bushes close by.

There were so many dragon and damsel flies hovering and weaving and diving all over the lake, that any random shot with some #8 birdshot from a twelve-gauge would've equaled a slaughter of the innocent Odonata insect order of a quantity enough to make an entomologist drop to their knees with tear-filled eyes. I'd seen it here on the lake like this before, but it had been a couple years at least. The last time it had been a trip I made with Jake, his younger brother hadn't come for some reason that's forgotten. We paddled around the lake and were entertained by bass splashing and performing feats of acrobatics in every direction as they did their best to fill up on the large insects.

There were so many that Jake actually knocked one out of the air while casting a marabou jig with his spinning reel. The air was just that thick with them. The irony being that the dragons and damsels were simply doing their best to lay eggs and ensure the survival of their species on the lake, all the while many of them meeting certain death.

Because I didn't see it every year, I knew like with most insects, it was all in the timing. And this year, our timing must have been right on again. I don't question these things much when I stumble upon them. I simply take advantage of them because like everything else in life, nothing lasts forever. You either use that time wisely or wonder how it *could have been* later on after it has passed. Right now, *I just wanted to get on the water*.

I paddled us out, not very far, and Nikki took the popper from the hook keeper and stripped out some line. I lined us up about twenty-five feet or so from some lily pads along the shore and told her to start casting when she was ready, and she made her first cast within about seven seconds. Apparently she was ready.

She missed a couple fish in the first few minutes. They'd take the popper and pull it under, but she couldn't get a good hook set. So I figured they were probably small fish, little bass or more likely bluegills that weren't big enough to even get the bass sized hook in their mouth. I was always amused that bluegills, or pumpkinseeds or any manner of sunfish for that matter, were so greedy that they'd try to eat something that never had a shot in hell of fitting in their little mouths.

Sometimes I wondered if they really didn't just have the little dog syndrome. You know...the little dogs always have the biggest attitudes. They bark and nip at anyone or anything like they don't have an understanding of how small they really are. They think they can intimidate you, and honestly, those little bastards usually do intimidate me. It's this little thing with these sharp gnashing teeth, and they move fast. And their eyes. How can something so small and cute be so frightening like a demon possessed kid's toy?

I wonder if the little pan fish aren't picking on that foam popper, grabbing its little rubber legs or the feather sticking out of its butt like a bully on a playground grabs a little girl's ponytail and laughs at her. They're just trying to push their non-existent weight around until you lift it from the water to make another cast somewhere else, at which point they probably think they ran it off and laugh and high-five each other.

The fish were still jumping all over the lake, but while you'd see a fish go completely airborne out in open water, the loudest commotions were literally right along the shore back in the tall grass. The long-bodied insects would land on the green blades to rest, only the fish were there waiting in the shallows, hidden in inches of water along the base of the tall grasses. They'd launch themselves up at their targets and thrash in the warm shallows, pushing through the grasses like a concert goer in a crowd using shoulders and elbows to move through it on the way to the beer stand.

It made sense to me that more attempts were being taken in the grass where the bugs were sitting still than out in the open where they were a constantly moving target, but the ratio wasn't over that big of a spread. I told her to try casting close to the grass, and not to worry about losing flies to the weeds. I was still working out of a popper box that had been tied a couple months ago for a bass guiding trip, so these flies were already paid for. Not to mention I still had quite a few. As soon as she placed her next cast closer to the shore, she brought her first bass to hand. After the first one they kept coming.

It was hot out. It had to be a little before noon, give or take, and none of the fish were monsters. Some of them, mostly largemouth bass, were less than ten inches. I always expect that in the warm shallows. But a fish is a fish. The way I see it, if you're catching small fish, it's better than missing a couple big fish and not catching anything at all. So at least starting with small fish is a good place to begin. I've always thought that you need to catch your first fish before you can catch the rest. It sounds blatantly obvious, I know; but in my head, I always tell myself after the first fish that *now it has fish stink on it.* Now, *it'll work.*

So Nikki was casting and catching, and it's always good to me to realize that you're at this specific point with someone. They were new at this once, not that they aren't still pretty green, but now you've arrived at that place where you don't have to do anything for them. You just put the paddle in the water every now and then to turn the canoe or move it to the next spot, and for the most part, they're sitting there casting and fishing, and so are you. You're not *helping* them fish, you're fishing *with them*.

She'd catch a bass and get it to the canoe, and maybe if she was struggling to remove the hook I'd scoot forward from the rear seat to get it. But for the most part, my part in the whole ordeal was simply taking a picture now and then or suggesting that she try casting to a certain spot, like the far side of those lily pads under that willow tree. At which point she'd say something with a smile, like *"Don't tell me what to do."* We were fishing. Both of us. It was great.

I was just working the perimeter of the lake, and we were

doing pretty decent. Ok, we were doing really well. In an hour we had probably caught a dozen or more bass ranging from eight inches up to probably fourteen or fifteen. The majority of the outer edges of the lake was a sudden stop of old hayfield that had, over the years, become brush and saplings mixed in with over hanging willow trees. The shore would come to an abrupt meeting with the water, and where the water began there would be a mix of weed beds and here and there patches of lily pads.

Most years, the weed beds were so thick that fishing anywhere within ten feet of the shore was impossible without some type of weedless fly, but not this year. For whatever reason, this year the weed beds were tight to the bottom, giving us more than enough water above them to fish poppers and even streamers if we felt so inclined. A guy at work tried to tell me that it was because it was a dry year. I must have looked at him like he was speaking some foreign language, I'm sure. I told him yeah, it was dry and hot...but the weed beds are UNDER WATER. He laughed. Somehow he was probably right, but it still seemed ridiculous to me.

Anyway, we'd come to the one side of the lake bordered by woods, and instead of lily pads and weed beds, there was a good ten feet of tall grass that bordered the shore here for about seventy-five yards. Out a few feet from that there was a sudden drop-off where the depth went from maybe four feet to over your head. If I'd been thinking about it, I would have also realized that the wind was blowing across the lake to this shoreline, and the biggest concentration of dragon and damsels was here - not to mention that sudden drop-off.

We hammered bass left and right as the canoe drifted parallel to the shoreline and we were having a blast. Every second or third cast was a bass, with an eight or nine-inch bluegill mixed in here and there. And then Nikki's popper was swallowed by a hole in the surface of the water that immediately stretched the leader and fly line out straight and down to the bottom.

She looked at me and pulled on the 7wt remembering to set

the hook good and then things got interesting fast. While largemouth bass in warm water aren't known as the biggest fighters, they're reliable enough to know that they're going to go straight down into whatever weeds they can find. This one had read the textbook and knew what was expected of it. Nikki was excitedly asking for advice and all I could tell her was *take it slow, don't break it off. If it wants to fight, let it fight, just keep tension.*

You know it's a decent fish when it changes the direction of the canoe, and this one did it three times at least. I had my long-handled net ready, and after missing it the second time the panic was there that we all get when we know it's about to be our fault that someone didn't land a good fish. No one wants that kind of thing hanging over their head.

For a couple months now, she'd been telling me that she wanted *a big boy*. She was completely happy just being out and fishing, which is all one can ever really hope for, but I knew she was really hoping to feel a really good fish on the end of her line. After all,...a*ren't we all?*

After the front of the canoe had swung in several different directions like the compass you just can't trust, she managed to bring the bass boat side and I scooped it up in the net. The yellow popper with the black stripes was firmly planted in the left side of its mouth, a textbook hook set. I couldn't help but notice while removing the popper that I could just about fit my closed fist in its mouth. The other thing I couldn't help but notice was the huge smile on Nikki's face. This was her first *good fish* on the fly. She wanted to feel a good fish on her line...*don't we all?*

21

Head Waters

A remote Adirondack canoe trip. It was one of those trips that will always stick out in my mind above the rest, always in the front, never in the back. I know that memories fade, and others can be made that can bump them down the list, but this wasn't one of those. This one will hold its position, no matter what else I do in the future. I'm pretty sure. My friends, they'll probably eventually roll their eyes right before they glaze over, because I'm so sure that this will be one of those trips I recount over and over again like a broken record anytime someone mentions canoe trips, or fishing in remote places, or talks about beavers and beaver dams.

JP and I took this trip with two new friends, Mike and Butch. Mike Crawford is a full-time guide, which these days is impressive enough. I couldn't imagine gambling my mortgage and monthly bills on hoping someone wanted to go fishing enough to pay me to take them. Mike lives the outdoors life I imagine most of us would love to. Of course, when it comes down to it, I just want to live my own outdoors life, while a full-time guide like Mike allows other people to live theirs. It's probably not a bad way to make a living. I'm not saying it's easy, I'm just saying there are probably worse ways to do it.

Then there's Butch Hassler, a seasoned Adirondack guide and Canadian Caribou guide; he's a personality, a genuine character. He's the guy that could be dropped into the wilderness with nothing but a shoelace and walk out three months later in a tuxedo and a smile. Although he has the skills, I also know him just well enough now that he'd probably forego the tux and simply show up in wool pants and bright orange suspenders. My kind of guy.

Oh, I lied. *Three new friends*. Butch's dog, Kelly, goes everywhere with him; and so, she accompanied us on this float as well, and I now consider her a friend, too. I'd like to think the feelings were mutual. Dogs are the best judge of character, so you should always strive to be sure that all dogs like you. It's a self-measuring tool that ranks right up there with another tool I use when I encounter any myriad scenarios in life...would my grandfather be proud of me? The way I figure it, if a dog likes you, and your grandfather would be proud, then you're doing it right.

As the crow flies, from put-in to take-out, the distance measured on a map was just over eight miles. 8.2, to be exact. But as Butch stated when I asked him how long he thought this float would actually be, he told us, *"Well, it's 8.2 miles as the crow flies. But the last time a crow tried to fly this river he got dizzy!"*

Having never met before the trip, I think both JP and I really weren't sure what to expect. We knew Mike was a guide because we learned that he'd guided someone on one of our favorite waters, a stream that Trout Power had discovered an unknown heritage brook trout strain on two years earlier. In all honesty, finding out that someone was guiding on the stream worried us a bit. We worried now that the watershed had recovered from the devastating effects of acid rain and that the fish had recovered on their own, that here would come the humans bent on exploiting it and ruin it again by trashing the place and fishing it out. But that's another story for another book.

We gave Mike a call to see if he knew the story of our research on the stream and what had been discovered, and he didn't. And he hadn't planned on guiding it anymore, it was merely an opportunity to stay at one of the old "Great Camps in the area" in his own words. It wasn't very long after our call to him that he sent us an email stating that not only was he completely on board with what Trout Power was doing, but he thought he had the next place to look for native fish that no one had yet recognized as native, heritage brook trout. If there were more out there, then after looking at the map, JP and I and the rest of the Trout Power board members agreed. This place was worth a look.

We met them for the first time at the take-out where we'd be leaving JP's Jeep. The plan was to leave JP and Mike's vehicles at the take-out so we'd have rides home at the end. A good friend of Butch's would drive us from there to the other end where we'd eventually portage in to begin the paddle. Mike and Butch were swapping packs and gear from Mike's truck into Butch's when we pulled into the take-out parking area. They both looked up and smiled.

A few days growth of salt and pepper facial hair - more salt than pepper - was my first observation of Mike besides his welcoming smile. He was doing something with a big dry bag, and he looked right at home. I suppose a guide should.

Butch was an older gentleman, wearing dark green wool pants and a button-up green wool shirt contrasted by wide, bright orange suspenders. He wore an old and weathered revolver on his side. Not like a gunfighter would wear a six shooter in a movie, more like any person might wear a Leatherman on their belt. I'm sure it would raise red flags with a good portion of today's population, but I don't consider myself as anything close to belonging to the bigger portion of today's population. And I don't look at that as a bad thing, either.

As we met and talked for the first few minutes, I knew almost immediately that Butch was sizing JP and I up, trying to decide if we were going to be up to this long paddle or if we were going to end up just a couple fisherman who had no idea what they were getting into; two guys that were going to end up wet and complaining for the next three days. More than once during the small talk, and while bags were being loaded into the truck, he mentioned to Mike how much "stuff you guys have" and that we still had two hours of driving to get to the land where we'd be portaging in. We needed to get moving. He was a man aware of what needed to be done and how. I took that as a good thing, wanting to get moving myself.

We portaged in to the headwaters of this river system, high above where anyone else ever floats, simply because Butch knew the land better than anyone else alive. Most paddlers would portage in from another lake and start miles downstream of where we were going to be starting. Mike told us ahead of time that Butch had been doing the float for years and years and that he knew it like the back of his hand. A lot of people claim to know places better than the back of their own hand. But listening to Butch talk about the place, I got the feeling that he wasn't a bullshitter. With some people you can just tell.

He was seventy-four years old and he'd been doing the float religiously for years now, with a group of like-minded friends. He told us that over the years, a couple friends had bowed out as time had went on, which was just one of those things that happens. Two years prior, one of his buddies did it for his last time. *I'd imagine anyways...*he was *eighty-nine*!

Normally their portage in was over three miles. This was the first opportunity for JP to make a good impression on Butch, without actually trying or realizing it. Simply put, no one wanted to portage in over three miles. We only had three days to do this. Who wants to spend an entire day getting to the water? I understand that *getting there is half the fun*, but on this particular trip if we could cut way down on the *getting there*, we'd have more time for fun after we got there. So to cut the portage down to a half mile, we tried contacting a private club.

It had seventy-five hundred acres that bordered the state land we were trying to access. During the initial trip planning, Mike mentioned that Butch had gotten permission to cut across the club land years ago and that there was a chance we'd be able to this time. That fell apart faster than it could have been put together. The club had let hikers and anglers do it in the past in hopes of gaining members, and when it hadn't worked they'd ended the practice completely. The only people gaining access to their land were members. Plain and simple.

JP is the guy who makes things happen. He saw an opportunity. He'd had a membership at another small club for years and wasn't happy with it. So he discontinued his membership with that one and became a member of this one. Just like that, with the click of an email, our canoe carry went from over three miles to a half a mile. I think everyone could appreciate that.

Friday afternoon, Butch's old friend Mark drove us from the take out to the Club property and we met some of the members. The president and vice president gave us a tour of the property while Mike and Butch drove the fourteen miles of dirt road across the club to unload two canoes and bushwhack to the put in. They wanted to scout out the way ahead of time, to save time on the way in the next morning.

That night we ate dinner in a hunting cabin with a small gathering of club members, the hospitality a warm welcome considering what we were about to tackle over the next three days. We ate a hot dinner at a table under a roof surrounded by walls and without bugs. What more could you ask for out here in the middle of nowhere? As you might expect, stories were told, and I saw Butch open up and come alive. He was one of the best storytellers I'd ever met. Everyone got quiet when he told a story and they normally ended with a burst of laughter that would shake windows.

We slept in an old logging bunkhouse that night. Mike stoked the woodstove and a bottle of Irish whiskey was produced out of Mike's pack. JP had brought one, of course, but it was shared and emptied at dinner with our generous hosts. After this night, it looked like it was up to me to supply the spirits for the next two nights. It was a good thing I'd packed light, light enough to make room for a couple turpentine cans of corn whiskey. Butch retired early to a bunk upstairs, while JP and Mike and I solved the world's problems one high ball glass at a time until there were no more to solve, and we turned out the lights.

The club members saw us off in the morning at the edge of the club's land. I think they may have thought we were a little crazy, watching two canoes with legs push through the undergrowth and disappear into the forest, two other characters with large dry bag packs leading the way, and a dog named Kelly wearing saddlebags coming and going from the scene. We all paused for a photo before we hoisted the canoes. Even Kelly sat at Butch's feet with her dog pack on. I'm pretty sure she smiled.

The portage took about an hour with Butch leading by GPS, Mike and I carrying the canoes, and JP shouldering a large assortment of packs and gear. It wasn't easy, but it was probably a hell of a lot easier than three miles and change. JP had shortened the portage with his membership and Butch didn't protest. He was grateful in the end, because as he put it, *being born at an early age was starting to catch up to him*. The portage wasn't the easiest, even after knocking a great distance off of it. But I've come to find in life that anything worth doing comes with challenges. If it didn't, everyone would be doing it. And then it really wouldn't be worth doing.

I welcomed the chance to carry a fifty-five-pound canoe on my shoulders for an hour through dense forest. Uphill, downhill, around fallen trees. A couple times we dragged them down steep grades. It was easier and safer to slide them down a steep grade of rotting leaves and fallen tree branches, less chance of twisting an ankle. I suppose I welcomed it for no other reason than every now and then you just have to prove to yourself that you can still push yourself, you can still *be pushed*, and hack it. Honestly, since I'd quit climbing cell towers a few years ago, I'd felt like there was a sense of adventure and challenge missing from life. I didn't push myself much anymore. I just assumed I still could. Out in the wilderness is *not* the place you want to confirm what they say the word *assume* does.

When we finally made it to the stream, Butch looked at me with approval. I wouldn't use the word *impressed*, but maybe *relieved*. I think he was relieved that we hadn't ended up being a couple of whiners, a couple green horns that couldn't hack the portage. Because if you couldn't hack an hour portage, how could you ever hope to hack the next three days in the wild?

The stream wasn't much to speak of. Butch told us it was

about as high in the head waters as you could get. Any higher would have brought us to an old mill that had been abandoned and taken back by the Adirondacks. A couple foundations and an old dam were the only evidence left. These were head waters, there was no doubt. When I say we began our float on a stream, I mean we began our float on a *stream*. The water was just barely wide enough for a canoe. Not much farther downstream it finally widened out to wide enough for two canoes side by side.

It branched out through a wide-open expanse of alders and tall grass; the odd, dead, gray sun-bleached pine stood lonesome here and there, trees that had been huge but in places that would have been more work than it was worth to cut down and haul out during the days of the logging boom. Silent giants. The remains of ancient sentinels of the great beaver meadow we were about to navigate.

Surrounded by hills and mountains, our float meandered through a huge (I guess this is as *good* a place and possibly the *best* place that I've ever had the opportunity to use the word *vast* to describe something)...it meandered through a *vast* beaver meadow. I've never been in one as expansive in my life. And if you know anything about streams that flow through high grass and alder-choked moose and beaver country, you might know that what Butch had stated earlier about dizzy crows is completely true. There were no straight stretches; it was a complex, confusing and disorienting flow, a never-ending series of hairpin turns and switch backs.

Once we were floating, there seemed to be no beginning and no end to the meadow, *it just existed*. We were merely intruders in no-man's land. It seemed as though there was no direction that a compass could point out in any certainty, dizzy crows indeed. Bend after bend, hardly a view except of the flanking hills colored in the peak fall foliage, their bottoms hidden behind the crowding alders and tall grasses. Above them the sky had no color at all, a washed out gray. I thought to myself a couple times that it appeared there was no sky at all.

Shortly after beginning the float, I spotted an old tall pine standing alone - still alive - a beautiful original growth tree in a land that had been mostly stripped of original growth a long time ago during the logging boom at the turn of the last century, and then again during the great blowdown of '95. I watched it slowly over the next couple hours get closer and farther away repeatedly, until finally passing under it almost two hours later. It was only a couple hundred yards away *several times*. But we'd make a series of bends at which point it would be farther away in a completely different direction, spotting it over the opposite shoulder that I'd last noticed it.

The alders that flanked the water were basically impenetrable, unless you were a beaver, in which case there seemed to be beaver tunnels and beaver slides hidden everywhere. The tunnels were nothing more than black voids where the water and alders met, something you might picture some Special Forces sniper team slowly emerging from with face paint and silent focus.

The slides came in from a foot or so above the water, smooth and muddy gaps in the undergrowth that came from nowhere and disappeared into wet nothing. I tried getting out of the canoe once and moving through the alders and high grass, then quickly decided it was probably a good way to end up cut up, frustrated, exhausted and hypothermic if anyone ever found themselves foolish enough to attempt a crossing on foot. The beaver and it's low center of gravity and the moose that towered above it all seemed the only plausible characters to traverse this terrain in any such story without a canoe. Which brings me to the second and most impressive obstacles. Beaver Dams.

Now I know I'm a fisherman. I'm very aware that the word of a fisherman is to be taken lightly, or to be taken with a grain of salt, or to be completely disregarded in some instances (for example, when hands are held out and the statement *"It was this big"* is uttered), but I want to express my sincerest intentions here that I'm not exaggerating when I tell you that we most likely dragged our canoes over *fifty beaver dams*. And that we most likely floated over or around *another twenty or so* that were either underwater or blown out on one end or the other. And there were a couple instances of large old growth pines in the couple wooded stretches that had blocked float passage. There we needed to either carry over, or in the least lie flat on our backs as if inventing some type of canoe limbo. In one limbo instance I realized that we were actually fortunate to be carrying the weight of our dry bags and fishing gear if for no other reason than taking that weight out would have made the canoes ride an inch higher...an inch that would have been the difference from carrying around or stuck underneath in a precarious situation.

It was serious work floating these headwaters, work I'd gladly dedicate myself to again tomorrow if the chance or need presented itself. I've been told numerous times over my life that beavers are no good for trout. I'm about to argue that here from experience, not just hearsay.

Now out there in the wide open, with no wooded flanks to shade the water from the heat of the sun, no cover except for tucking under the alders against the banks, there'd be no structure; and with no structure, no oxygen being churned in the water. I understand that merely one or two beaver dams wouldn't do much of anything to improve this as a brook trout habitat. That being said, *fifty or so dams* on the other hand not only creates fifty or so small deeper pools to find cooler water on the very bottom, but it creates fifty or so miniature unnatural *waterfalls* producing pockets of white churning water on the downstream of these dams.

In my head, calling the dams "unnatural" starts a debate. Because on one hand, if it wasn't for a large beaver population building them, Mother Nature herself wouldn't have put them there. It would've been a slow and meandering, almost *stillwater*. But on the other hand, I'd say that the beavers are *indeed and actually Mother Nature at work*, part of her design, and therefore *indeed natural*. It's a rabbit hole you could go down if you like. I'll just accept it for what I saw it as. Beavers creating excellent brook trout waters.

Not only were the brook trout there in great numbers, but being fall and just before spawning, they were aggressive. How aggressive? Well, I always fish them with small streamers, so to say that they were chasing down streamers really doesn't reinforce the claim. To me, that's just normal. Instead, I'll use Mike's fishing tactics to illustrate.

He was fishing a small bugger/nymph looking thing under an indicator, a ball of foam. You know, the two-toned red and bright yellow foam indicators that are about the size of small bass popper. More than once he made a cast and almost instantly or while moving the rig to another spot those brookies were coming up and trying to eat that indicator!

Butch hadn't brought a fishing rod. I thought it odd at first, then I discovered...*Butch doesn't fish*. Let me explain. When I asked how it was possible that he could float this river every year and be such an outdoorsman as he was but *not fish*, he volunteered an answer matter-of-factly.

When he was a kid, his mother would tell him to get dinner. That meant go catch fish. It was a chore, *not* done for fun. So he grew up looking at it differently than most of us and in turn, never viewed it as anything more than a chore. He's enough of an outdoorsman, one who can outdo just about all of us in any wilderness skill needed out there, so I let the whole non-fisherman thing slide. I let it slide, but I still couldn't grasp the idea myself. Mowing the lawn was a chore, so I didn't do it, hardly even half as much as my neighbors anyways. But fishing? I let it slide but couldn't grasp the concept.

Butch didn't fish. So I laughed at his comments about Mike fishing the indicator. After the third hard strike at the indicator, Butch told Mike *"You need to put a hook on your bobber!"* Naturally, Mike corrected him. *"It's not a bobber, Butch, it's an indicator."* To which I added *"Yes, this is fly fishing Butch. It's much too sophisticated to use bobbers."*

The brookies were everywhere in the headwaters, our timing seemed to be dead on. Their colors were only beginning to pop.

Where the tree's leaves were at their peak, the brookies were only every so often at theirs. They'd obviously made their way upstream to get ready to spawn but weren't actually ready yet.

I began fishing before we ever even put the canoes in motion. I caught a small five-inch brookie from a slow and dark run above a beaver dam about fifty yards upstream of where we readied the canoes. In my mind, casting a line where we were going to first put paddle to water wasn't enough. I had to catch something *upstream*. Just to say I did. I caught one and saw the copper flashes of two others; and even if I hadn't managed the one, I'd have been happy enough to see them. It's always a comfort to miss a fish but to see it. Then at least you know it was there, rather than to get completely skunked and wonder if you're casting to nothing for the rest of the day.

Downstream as we paddled on, fish took my tiny streamer pattern; they took Mike's bead headed bugger pattern, and then after they began to attack his indicator, they ferociously pummeled his *Big Humpy* dry fly. They didn't seem to care if they were taking a bug off the surface or a streamer underneath, which has always been my general observation on brook trout, really. Even when you see one rising to bugs now and then, which seems less common than brown trout rising to bugs, they'll usually still take a streamer. Which is nothing like most browns, the fish that won't take the perfect pattern for the hatch because it's a size too big or too small on many occasions.

Likewise, where a brown will get spooked and get lock jaw from too much commotion, the brook trout act more like bass in the fact that it seems to attract them. To a point. Now, I've seen pike attack a small stick thrown in the water. I'm not saying brook trout are that fearless or aggressive, don't get me wrong. But they certainly don't act like brown trout. In the Adirondacks we have a way of fishing dries that seems to be foreign to a lot of other locations. You can drift a dry, sure. Match the speed of the current, match the drift, match the hatch, mend lines, and focus on the most natural presentation you can present. But when it comes to brook trout in the Adirondacks, skating a dry across the surface is like one of those triangle dinner bells being rung on the old homestead. JP loves to say that when you're fishing for brookies, *just do everything the opposite of what you'd do for browns*. It's pretty sound advice.

Our first day on the river, we paddled and fished for two hours before we came to the spot Butch wanted to stop for a snack and a stretch. It was the put in, the end of the portage that everyone else used to start their float on the river. We'd started on the water two hours above where everyone else started. That put a smile on my face. Mike used a paddle as a cutting board for some cheese and sausage, and after a few stories about the area on some of Butch's past floats, we were on our way again. Mike managed a couple more brookies from the landing before setting back down in the canoe. Casting from hard ground had suddenly become a luxury one didn't pass up.

It rained on our first night. It drizzled most of the day, but shortly after we all climbed into our tents that night, the rain began to fall harder. Just before it began to sound like heavy static electricity on our tents, there was a loud and startling crash in the distance. Somewhere a tree fell. Now I've heard trees fall like that before, and my first thought is always something along the lines of, *"Well, that answers that question."* But when you really think about it, nope, it doesn't. We heard it, because we were there. So the question of "If a tree falls in the forest and no one is around to hear it, does it make a sound?" remains unanswered. But it wasn't close to us, so I can at least tell you that if a tree falls in the forest and you're being quiet and it doesn't know you're there, it still makes a sound.

In the morning, I wondered out loud if it could have been a beaver at work. Everyone nodded in agreement. Butch added, "Probably as likely as a dead tree finally falling out there somewhere." I'd have to speculate that if we had the answers to everything, life would be boring. And having all the answers would make us even dumber, if you ask me.

The next day was spent mostly paddling. We caught a few fish first thing, and then the fishing just turned off, the way fishing does sometimes. At first that's what I chalked it up to, the fishing just *turning off*. But the farther we paddled, the more I thought about how much different the river looked now. It was twice the width, deeper, not a tiny stream anymore.

A day earlier, crossing a beaver dam meant I'd jump out of the front of the canoe and stand in thigh deep water to pull the boat over. Then I'd hop back in and we'd be on our way around the bend to the next one. Before we'd nose up to a dam, we'd hang back and make a few casts and catch some trout. A lot of the time we'd make a few casts from the dam to the water below it too. It had worked.

On the second day, about the time the fishing *turned off* is about the time I started realizing the difference at the beaver dams. I couldn't just hop out and hop off the beaver dam anymore. I had to look for structure to stand on while pulling the canoe over, and then climb my way up into the alders and grass to get back into the canoe. The water was a lot deeper. Deep enough that I had to worry about stepping off the dams and going for a swim.

As the fishing turned off, we found ourselves moving downstream slower, only because we were spending more time casting, looking for fish, and not catching them. Which leads to more casting, hoping your luck will change, that the bite will turn on. Which leads to more time. It finally hit me that maybe the fish had all moved into the headwaters to spawn and that there just weren't any here now. Maybe we'd gone far enough downstream to leave them behind.

After eating cheese and sausage and beef jerky off another paddle cutting board, we decided that we'd caught enough fish, and there was too far to go to get to the end the following day for us to keep lollygagging around, casting to fish that were no longer there. Butch seemed a little concerned that we were moving a little too slow. He knew where we wanted to camp that night and knew how far we still had to go, so we paddled the rest of the day, only making a handful of casts to places that just looked too good to pass up. We paddled for a solid seven hours on day two. My shoulders burned slightly. I felt alive.

When we reached the place called High Falls, we came into contact with the first people we'd seen since we left the club property, and a sudden feeling of melancholy came over me. For so many miles, for two days, we'd had no company but each other and the silence and thoughts in our own heads. And the fish, birds, and the beavers that we knew were there but never saw, and the same with the moose and deer and bears. But here at High Falls, a quick portage around a twenty-foot waterfall was all that was needed to remind me that the older I get, the more I hate people.

There was a campsite off to the side of the falls, up top, a lean-to put there by the state so that all who ventured to find the falls could stay the night under shelter. It seems like a nice enough idea. And it is. But after floating for countless miles and seeing no a trace of humans, that first beer can and abandoned water bottle sunken in the pool above the falls is a major downer. And of course, there was a family staying at the lean-to. I'd never hold anything against a husband and a wife bringing their young son to such a place, but it would be a huge letdown after the isolation and privacy of the previous night. Plus, it just meant moving on another couple hours down river to the next campsite, hoping it wasn't taken. It only started there.

Past the lean-to, before the trail started down to the put-in, there was a trail intersection. I had to do a double take when I saw the young man, college age, with his fedora hat and tight pants pulled up to his shins... and bare feet. I wanted to punch him in the face for looking like someone out attempting to find his place in the world, while looking completely lost and out of touch with any reality.

He probably had some pot and mushrooms in his little canvas pack. But no socks. As we passed, JP smiled and nodded saying "Hello, how's it going?" Something unintelligible came in reply, as if this hipster couldn't be bothered with such mundane conversation. At that moment, I hoped to see him stub a bare toe or step on a pointy rock. I suddenly remembered. I hate people.

At the bottom of the falls, we caught up to Butch and Mike, where another canoe from downstream was pulling up to the landing. This place was suddenly like a damn airport, people coming and going everywhere. Kelly trotted to the landing to say hello and the woman in the front of the canoe started yelling *NO!* at her, panicking and trying to push her canoe back out with the paddle. The man in the rear rolled his eyes and grabbed the collar of the dog between them as the woman continued to voice her excited concerns. *"She just doesn't get along with other dogs! Get your dog away from us!"*

Butch calmly called Kelly back to him. She turned away from the canoe and walked over with a long face. Butch asked them how many other people they'd seen down river, if they'd noticed people at other lean-tos. I didn't hear their answer; I didn't want to hear anything they had to say. They headed back downstream. I assumed to try to beat us to the next open campsite. I knew they were just paddlers, people out enjoying the great outdoors, but they'd crossed my path after two days of no human contact, something I find myself avoiding more and more the older I get. I turned and saw the hipster with no shoes headed back up the trail behind us, then looked back downstream at the departing canoe. Busy as an airport? I thought of the old bumper sticker, *"If assholes could fly..."*

Our last campsite was only about two and a half hours from the take-out. We'd meant to stop and camp sooner, but there were people everywhere now. We were close enough to civilization that paddlers were common. Most were friendly enough, but the world is a big place with a lot of people these days. And it's just simple reasoning that the more people there are, the more assholes there will eventually be.

We passed a lone kayaker, a woman around fifty if I was guessing. Butch waved and asked her if she'd noticed anyone downstream at the next lean-to when she'd passed it. In a French-Canadian accent she told him that she hadn't seen a lean-to. Butch smiled and told her, *"Oh, you would have passed it about twenty minutes ago probably, on the right side."* She shrugged her shoulders, made a rude expression and told him, "Well then I guess I don't know if there's anyone there." As she passed our canoe I nodded and smiled, and she rolled her eyes and shook her head. Maybe she was just as upset at seeing others on the water as I was now, but I still smiled and faked it. Yep. The more people, the more assholes, I figured.

That night we got a good fire going, which I didn't think we'd be able to do as wet as everything was. But Butch and I gathered the best wood we could find and managed a great fire. Mike cooked us a great dinner of rice and caribou and Kelly laid down in the ferns back from the fire. She passed out as comfortably as any dog in a house would on the living room floor. It was one final night of telling stories, passing around a little whiskey, and wishing we were farther upstream still miles from any other human beings.

The next morning while the water was heating for some oatmeal, I did manage one brook trout. It was a welcome catch to start the day off right, knowing we'd be back in JP's Jeep before lunch, with emails and text messages pinging away as soon as we were back in range of cell service.

All in all, for what was 8.2 miles as the crow flies, we ended up actually floating about thirty miles. There are too many lessons learned on a trip like that. Because of where you went, who you went with, and everything you saw. Probably more learned and forgotten than I can remember. You know, the things you learn along the way that you didn't know before, and then they're gone. Until one day you're in some situation or thinking about something else and it just pops back in your head.

Like mushrooms. I learned once from a good friend what wild mushrooms I could eat without dying. Only after a while of not needing to eat any wild mushrooms because there's always something else to eat, I forgot what I'd learned from him. Until a discussion around the fire that last night with Mike and Butch and JP about mushrooms, then I remembered.

My good friend, Chris O'Bryan, was telling me once which mushrooms (should I need a meal in a hairy situation) were ok to eat. But I caught on that as he described a couple different ones, he'd say they were *"usually"* ok to eat. *"Usually"* I asked? *"So, what are you supposed to do? Take a little bite and wait and see?"* "Of course not," he said. "You give it to your friend first and wait and see. Never eat a mushroom you're not sure of!"

Who knows what lessons I learned along this float will end up popping up in my head at later dates? I know it'll happen, it always does. But there *were two* that stick out like the cliché sore thumb.

One: Contrary to my previous beliefs, beavers are not always bad for trout. They can actually improve things under the right circumstances. And two: You *CAN* trust a man who doesn't fish. Every now and then. One out of a hundred. Ok, maybe one out of a thousand. If their name is Butch. And they have a dog named Kelly that loves canoe trips.

22

Matters of Importance

The creek out back. That's how I refer to it most of the time. It has a name like most creeks, but to me it's the creek out back. Why? Because that's where it is. The name isn't important on most days. Less and less becomes important to me all the time the older I get it seems. And what I hold onto as *actually* important likewise becomes more important the older I get. The creek is important. Its name, not so much as its location. Out back.

Out back I can take the boys and we can spend a couple hours together fishing, talking or not talking. But they're nine and fourteen, so there's usually talking. Carter can ramble on about nothing at all out of nowhere the way most nine-year-olds can, and he does. He's at that age where everything can be funny and he's just learning to be a wise-ass. He loves to come up with the most outlandish statements just because he needs to be talking, and if he's talking I think he figures he may as well get your attention. And if you challenge some outlandish idea, he only answers the challenge with another matter of fact sarcastic wise crack. If he's not lost in thought while he's casting, this is what he's doing while his older brother is concentrating on putting his cast on a pinpoint target somewhere within ear shot. That is, until he gets a fish on. *Then* Carter is all business.

Carter is all about holding the fish. While his older brother Jake would rather not, Carter *needs* to hold the fish. There's something inside him that connects him to the whole experience through holding that which lives in another world apart from ours. Trapped below a clear barrier that is the surface of the water, the fish are a thing of fascination to him. Like most of us, I can see it in his eyes. When he holds a fish, he studies it. It's a great thing for him to come into contact with it. Jake, I think looks at the fishing like he does baseball or basketball. He is there for the challenge more than the fish itself. Although I know for a fact it slows his mind down, the same as mine.

The creek was *ok* last year. We caught smallmouths, we caught decent sized fallfish, and we had cruising carp pass us moving up and downstream while we stood in shin-deep runs. Jake actually caught a few more fish than Carter, which was good in my mind. It balanced out Carter's enthusiasm for the catch with Jake's business-like approach to the affair. And since Jake would rather not hold the fish most of the time and it's all Carter wants to do, it brings two brothers together in a way most other things can't.

While they might get in arguments about a video game and whose fault it was that someone lost, or while they fight about who was safe or out at first base, when Jake catches a fish and Carter releases it there's no doubt as to who did what and that they did it together. The creek out back seems to be the one sure place where they're brothers the entire time they're on it.

I'm not extremely close to my younger siblings. I feel bad about it most of the time, but it's just the way life has worked out. They're a lot younger than me; they were only just getting interesting as I left home for the military twenty-four years ago, and upon coming home a lot of time and growing up had happened in between. I moved away. They grew up. I moved back, they moved away. My brother Luke stayed around, but as life has its ways of doing, we've chosen our own paths, and adult responsibilities pretty much keep us busy in our own directions. But there's always the pond next to the house we grew up in that I look back on when I look at Jake and Carter on the creek together.

The pond was less than an acre, shaped like most man-made ponds. Mostly round and elongated, a couple willow trees overhung it on the far side back then, and it was fed by a spring, a stream that ran off of another property up the road. It was shallow and weedy on the end where the stream flowed in, but on the end where the water exited, it was supposedly twelve feet deep. We couldn't see the bottom so for all we knew it was true. It could've been twenty.

While we didn't always get along together in the house, once we were standing on the side of the pond with fishing poles in hand, we became a team. We stalked bass and when one was closer to someone else we quietly pointed them out to the nearest sibling like a big game hunter guide might point out a specific water buffalo on a safari to a client. We caught bait together and discussed which way was the best way to rig a live frog so that a bass would be hooked.

We had our own personal fishing poles, but the tackle boxes in the shed were for anyone to use. And while we might rush to open it first to get to that one lure we wanted before someone else, we never argued over who was using what; at least that I can remember now. That seems a little bit unrealistic, but as I said before, as I get older some things become less important and others more. And arguing when we were kids doesn't seem to have any importance to me today. Conversely, the fact that we fished together what seemed like almost every day of the summer is very important to me these days.

I'll never forget the day my brother Luke got stabbed in the palm of his hand by a bullhead's fin spine. It's a feeling you don't forget if you've never had it happen to you, best described as a quick and sharp pain that ends with a long lasting burning sensation. If I was sixteen or seventeen, then Luke was ten or eleven. He went back to the shed and returned with a heavy work glove and wouldn't touch another one without the glove on for a long time. A year or two later, I left for the Air Force.

While I was away in Texas in basic training, my mother had sent me an envelope with some photos in it from back home. I still have those photos today. It's funny, I set up my new writing area in my new house and I've tried to keep it pretty clean and uncluttered. I covered a wall with red barn clapboard siding to separate my writing area apart from everything else. I placed a desk against the wall, and a small antique fly chest full of drawers out of an old store. It's relatively neat and uncluttered. A couple large framed fish photos and a dictionary and thesaurus, and a mounted rooster. The first items speak for themselves and the latter is simply because I couldn't escape suburbia hell as I'd intended. A mounted rooster seems to me somehow an appropriate form of protest.

Anyway, there's one old photo hung with its corner stuck between the old red barn wood siding pieces. An old Polaroid sent to me while I was in basic training. On the back is written Luke 8-'94. I never got the significance of it until just recently, some twenty-five years later. I hadn't been gone for all that long, yet in that picture, he was holding a really nice bullhead in the photo...with no glove.

Most of us grew up on the water to some extent, those of us who claim to be anglers. Some of us had camps on lakes, some of us had parents with boats, and a lot of us just had parents that took us fishing or allowed us to trek off to ponds with friends so that we could be children. Some of us were lucky enough to have that pond close by.

I don't remember arguing on the pond, even though there's no way it didn't happen. I guarantee there were plenty of times that someone went stomping off back to the house to tell on someone else for something. It's not important. What's important is the memory of my brother getting struck in the hand with a bullhead's fin spine and realizing that after I'd left he kept growing up on the pond, the proof was in that photo.

The most important time in our lives is probably childhood. It's the only place that I know of I can go back to that's a place I can only get to if I have a fishing rod in my hand or put one in my son's. Somethings become less important as you get older, and others become more so.

There's always places we'd rather be, and always times we'd like to go back to. All that means is you once did the right thing in the right place at the right time. People will tell you don't look back. They love to say that. I don't know how many times I heard that. Don't look back, look ahead. I say go ahead, look back. Just choose what you look back at wisely.

Epilogue

I look back all the time. People say don't look back, but I've never been able to look forward as easy as back. I suppose that's why I've always held grudges, and most likely why I've always felt like I've been spinning my wheels for a good portion of my life. I've never been good at letting things go.

Of course, it comes in handy each time I sit down to write. I might not be able to remember what I was doing three hours ago, but I can remember stuff I did *"way back when."* Because I don't ever let go of anything. Like fishing for Walleye on Fish Creek at my great aunt and uncle's camp when I was probably no more than three or four years old. The people who owned the camp next door had an Irish Setter named Rusty, and they flew remote controlled pontoon planes that they took off and landed on the river. I can't remember today what I had for lunch yesterday, but I can remember the old 1950s camper with the addition built on the side of it where my aunts and uncles and cousins would sit and play cards some forty years ago.

Perhaps that's why I write, because I remember it all, but know that someday my mind will go and it'll all be gone. Maybe I'm trying to save what I can knowing nothing lasts forever.

Twenty something years ago, I was on the shore of Lake Arrow Head in Texas. A foot away a small fire was burning in the middle of a likewise small ring of rocks, a pile of scrounged wood (most likely mesquite from what I could tell) was gathered off to the side. (We didn't have mesquite in N.Y.). It was cold, and I knew there was never going to be enough wood to keep the fire going through the night. I rolled up in a wool blanket that I'd pulled from my dorm room closet back on base and covered my face with a knit hat. I remember thinking how much warmer my own breath felt on my face trapped under the blanket than the fresh night air. And I can still hear the voices of the other guys I was with as I drifted off to sleep. *"How the hell can he sleep out here like this!? He's nuts. We better get some more wood."*

The next morning, I woke up and pulled the wool from my eyes to find a light dusting of snow covering everything, including me. The other guys I was with all stood along the water's edge with their backs to me looking out over the lake, swaying in place, their arms crossed over their upper bodies and hands rubbing their biceps trying to remember what it felt like to feel warm. Their breath hung in the air in front of them like the steam that rises from factory smoke stacks, carrying away and finally dissipating into nothing.

The tallest one, his name was Thompson, turned to see me and walked over. Even though there were four of us out there, Thompson is the only one I can remember today. He was tall and lanky, and spoke in a southern drawl. I'll never forget the day I saw him get mail from home and I questioned the address. *"Wait a minute, you're from a town called Cut and Shoot?"* He confirmed it, he was from Cut and Shoot, Texas, a tiny town with barely a thousand people in it, and it was named after a fight at a church or something along those lines. That's probably why I remember him out of everyone there. You just don't forget something like that.

Anyway, Thompson walked over and kicked the ashes in the fire with the toe of his boot; there wasn't so much as a single red coal left. Ash dust billowed around his boot and settled back down like the particles in a snow globe. *"The fire died hours ago, none of the wood we could find on the ground would hardly burn with the snow and all. We were going to wake you up to leave, but nobody wanted to touch you. They thought you might be dead."* He chuckled. I grinned, stood up and re-wrapped the wool blanket over my shoulders and looked down to where I'd been sleeping. Snow covered everything except the perfect outline of where my body had been.

Thompson just stared at me. *"I don't know how the hell you slept like that, but I guess you Yankees are tougher than we think."* I still hadn't gotten used to the idea that I was in a place where even though I was in the same country, people thought of me as something other than just American. I grinned again, for a lack of anything else to reply with. Then he said, *"You're going to end up like Crocodile Dundee just living off the minimum someday, aren't you?"*

That's honestly the only conversation I can remember having with Thompson besides the one about Cut and Shoot, Texas. I was nineteen years old. And that sentence has echoed in my mind ever since then. How I ended up a slave to the machine is beyond me.

Today I spin my wheels like the majority of the population, trying to make ends meet. Trying to keep the mortgage payments going out. Trying to put money aside for a newer vehicle as the Jeep is almost twenty years old. It's starting to act like a grumpy eighty-year-old man who finds himself saying, *"I'm getting to old for this shit"* more and more often. I put a cylinder head on the motor in the fall. If it were an old man, it would have been like a lung transplant or maybe a bypass. *"You'll feel better after this sir, but you're going to need to slow down. You can't do all the things you used to do anymore, and the things you still can will take longer."* I'm always waiting for the next failure and am afraid to drive it very far anymore.

I work to keep my little parcel of suburbia hell with the lawn I hate to mow and the creek out back from falling into the hands of some bank eighteen-hundred miles away. I think I've always known it, but during the duration of my divorce and the time it took to finish my second book it really hit home with me.

The job and most of the jobs in the past. The house. The lawn and what the rest of the world thinks is important enough to be shackled to the idea of working their life away for. None of it matters to me. I'm pretty sure I've always known it, but I got married and we believed that we had to have the house and the white picket fence with two cars in the driveway and cable TV and a nice living room set and on and on. Honestly none of it has *ever* mattered to me. It never has, but I still fell into the trap all the same, trying to make someone else happy. And here I am with my foot in the trap, the trap staked to the ground.

In the spring of 2018, I was supposed to go to Argentina to fish for golden dorado. The opportunity came about because of a group of fishing lodges down there all banding together to form an organization of lodges working towards conservation and keeping the money made from fishing their waters in the pockets of the locals. I was asked if I'd be interested in editing their English website, if I'd take what they had translated into English and make it flow better so that it would read well to those from out of the country whose first language was English. It was a nice distraction while living in Chris and Kelly's basement; it made me feel like I was still worth something at one of the lowest points in my life.

I was supposed to go down and fish for golden dorado in May, see it for myself. It would've literally been checking a fish and a location off my bucket list. But a couple months before I was to go, my depression got the best of me and I cancelled it altogether. I had lots of excuses. Chris and JP were both pushing me, Chris threatened to physically harm me if I didn't take advantage of such an offer the way I remember it. And JP and John Montefusco were beside themselves that I was going to bail on it. Out of all the excuses I made, the only one that I thought was really true was a lie I told myself. *Guys like me don't get to do trips like that.*

I was so far removed from anything good at the time that it really didn't affect me much when the time came and went. But now, with the opportunity a year behind me, regret stings like a bare hand on a hot woodstove. You knew it was hot but did it anyway, and now you feel like a moron.

I would've been gone for twelve days. That's really not that long. I'm forty-three years old now. Twelve days never seemed like much. I mean, how much is a week when it's considered over an entire lifetime? Not much...until you find yourself halfway through life or more for all you know. I've realized I should be making every week count. I suppose every day really. I guess it's something some people don't learn until they get older. How old? Well, I don't know. But I'm just now realizing it, and I've never been this old before. So I guess for me it's about this old.

Fishing always was, and now fly fishing *specifically,* has become my escape from what everyone else seems to think is normal and necessary. I'm looking forward lately. Ten to twelve years. When the boys are making their way into the world, I'll take a chance and try to remake mine. I'll sell the house, maybe move out west somewhere to work in a fly shop where I make just enough money to rent some tiny apartment because that's all I need. Or maybe I'll just buy a really nice backpack and strap a small arsenal of fly rod tubes to it and start walking. With no child support and no real responsibilities, I could pretty much wander off and do whatever I felt like doing. And you can bet that *wouldn't* be the lawn. There are fish to catch in any direction I might go. I think Crocodile Dundee called it a *walk-about.*

Until then, I'm going to try to figure out life. How to make it work for me with the cards I've been dealt. Some things you have to learn the hard way. I'll be correcting these mistakes for a while. I guess that's *why* it's called the hard way. I've led most of my life with a level of uncertainty when I really look back at it. Nothing was ever calculated, it was just each day as it came. No looking forward, always looking back. I've come to grips with the fact that there really isn't anything certain in life, as much as we all wish and try to tell ourselves that there is. The only certainty I've found is that at the end of every cast, there may or may not be a fish. And you never know until you make that cast.

Make the cast.

You may also enjoy...

Reflections of a Fly Rod

By Mark Usyk

www.ingramcontent.com/pod-product-compliance
Lightning Source LLC
Chambersburg PA
CBHW021947290426
44108CB00012B/986